Mapping America:

A Guide to Historical Geography

Second Edition

Volume 2

Ken L. Weatherbie
Del Mar College

LONGMAN

An Imprint of Addison Wesley Longman, Inc.

New York • Reading, Massachusetts • Menlo Park, California • Harlow, England
Don Mills, Ontario • Sydney • Mexico City • Madrid • Amsterdam

Mapping America: A Guide to Historical Geography, Second Edition, Volume II by Ken L. Weatherbie.

Copyright © 1998 Longman Publishers USA, a division of Addison Wesley Longman, Inc.

ISBN: 0-321-00488-4

CB

98 99 00 01 02 9 8 7 6 5 4 3 2 1

Mapping America

CONTENTS - VOLUME 2

Preface

Preface

Mapping America: A Guide to Historical Geography is designed to provide a review of American geography and an introduction to the important role that the topography and geography of this continent has played in the history of the United States.

This workbook presents the basic geography of the United States—the places and river systems—so that students can place the history of the United States into spatial perspective. Sites and names serve as reference points for the rest of American history; unless one is very clear that Charleston is in South Carolina and Charlestown is in Massachusetts, some parts of the Revolutionary War can be quite confusing. A secondary objective of this workbook is to teach, and reinforce through practice, reading visual material as historical documents. The reference maps included here may be analyzed and interpreted much like a primary textual source—a speech or a letter—in order to glean information about the past. The third objective is to connect these maps to the historical period under consideration.

Keep the following two questions in mind while working on the exercises in this workbook.

From what point of view is the map drawn? Maps are drawn from one perspective or another. For example, each country usually puts itself in the middle of a world map. Think of how accustomed we are to seeing the Europe and the United States right smack in the middle of the world and how odd it would seem to have Australia in the center. Maps of the United States usually show Texas at the bottom, California on the left, and Maine on the right. They could just as well show Texas at the top—but that would look upside down. All map, like all documents, reflect choices about what is more important and what is less important.

Furthermore, one must remember that maps are always inadequate representations of geography—no two-dimensional image can ever fully and accurately reproduce the three-dimensional sphere of the earth. Traditionally, map makers have used a modification of the Mercator projection in which the earth is projected into a cylinder. This type of projection is very distorted, however, particularly in that the areas around the poles appear to actually be much larger than they are (Greenland isn't really that big). The Mercator projection is only truly accurate in estimating areas and distances close to the equator.

What scale is shown on the map? As the shortcomings of the Mercator projection show, maps can be deceptive so scale is vitally important. If a map doesn't have a scale indicating how many inches (or centimeters) represent how many miles (or kilometers), compare it to another map. Are there differences? Remember how much bigger the western American states are than most eastern states, for example, or how small Europe really is as opposed to the other continents. Scale can also be very important to notice in historical maps of demographics, or population growth—a large city in 1750 isn't in the same ballpark as a large city in 1997 although maps may portray them as such.

The maps in this workbook are divided up into three sections, each with a brief introduction setting the context for the map exercise. On the opposing pages are questions in three categories:

Mapping America presents labeling and drawing exercises designed to review basic locations and spatial relationships.

Reading the Map includes a set of fill-in-the-blank questions that can be answered by studying the outline map and your textbook(s).

Interpreting the Map poses a series of general questions connecting geography with the historical era under consideration.

Text references and answers to the fill-in-the-blank and interpretive questions are provided in the back of this book.

It is our hope that *Mapping America* will improve your ability to read and interpret maps and will help you better understand and appreciate American history.

MAPPING EXERCISES

CHAPTER 1

THE CIVIL WAR

The Civil War, fought between 1861 and 1865, saw armies of unprecedented size engaged in bloody combat over a vast expanse of territory. Necessarily, the terrain influenced the grand strategies and field tactics of both sides. The maneuvering of armies, the transport of supplies, and the locations of battles were often determined by geographical factors. The Union victory was in part a result of its skillful consideration of the natural and constructed environments.

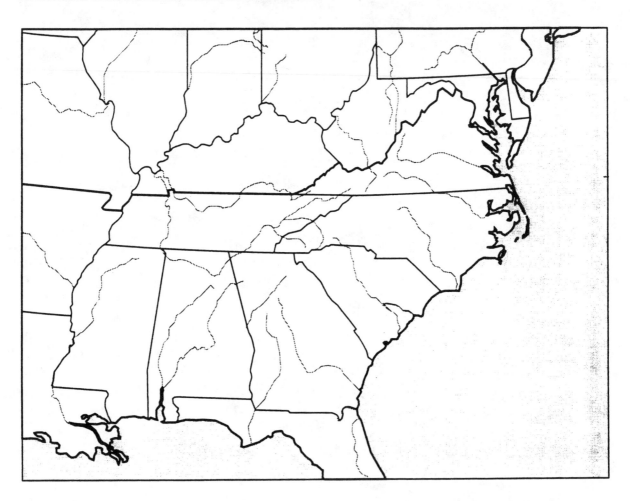

CHAPTER 1

MAPPING AMERICA

1. Locate with an X, then label: Gettysburg, Richmond, Antietam, Bull Run, Vicksburg, New Orleans, Ft. Henry, Ft. Donelson, Shiloh, Atlanta, Chattanooga, Savannah, Washington, D.C., Appomattox.
2. Label: Ohio, Mississippi, Potomac, York, Cumberland, and Tennessee Rivers; Chesapeake Bay; Shenandoah Valley; Appalachian Mountains.
3. Draw an arrow to indicate the path of Sherman's March to the Sea.
4. Mark some of the major industrial areas, transportation routes, and urban areas in the United States before the Civil War.

READING THE MAP

1. The Peninsula campaign refers to the Union effort to seize _____ by invading it from the east along the peninsula formed by the _____ River and the _____ River.
2. The two major Civil War battles fought on Union soil were at _____ and _____.
3. The Union strategy to "divide and conquer" the Confederacy led to two lines of invasion. The first ran along the line of the _____ River, and the second along the _____ River. A third line of invasion, with an emphasis on "conquer" rather than "divide," was Sherman's march from _____ to _____.
4. The Union gained an important naval victory at the key southern port of _____ in 1862, but won virtual control of the Mississippi River only with the siege of _____, completed in mid-1863.
5. The first Union victories in the Civil War were at Forts _____ and _____ in western Tennessee, but their advance was blunted by Confederate defenses at _____.
6. The Union's resource advantages included _____, _____, and _____. The Confederate advantages included _____, _____, and _____.

INTERPRETING THE MAP

1. What geographical fact meant that a great deal of the fighting of the Civil War would be in northern Virginia?
2. Why was Tennessee a state of key strategic importance in the Civil War?
3. The Confederacy had no real navy. What geographical feature of the Confederacy blunted the impact of that deficiency?
4. Contrast the transportation and industrial systems in the North and South. How did locations of important transportation lines or industrial sites affect military strategy in the Civil War?

CHAPTER 2

RAILROADS AND NEW TRANSPORTATION SYSTEMS

The late nineteenth century saw an explosion of new railroads criss-crossing the American continent. A network of 30,000 miles of track in 1860 grew to include more than 190,000 miles of track by 1900. The early railroad system was a complex and inefficient one incorporating more than ten different rail gauges—meaning trains had to be unloaded and reloaded every time the track switched. After the Civil War, however, large monopolies began to dominate and buy up smaller railroads, and a standard gauge was adopted in 1886. The large railroads, financed by the government and the great corporations that managed them, spurred industrial development and helped introduce new economic and social patterns across the United States. They also drastically changed the American environment. More than anything, they opened up the West and closed the frontier.

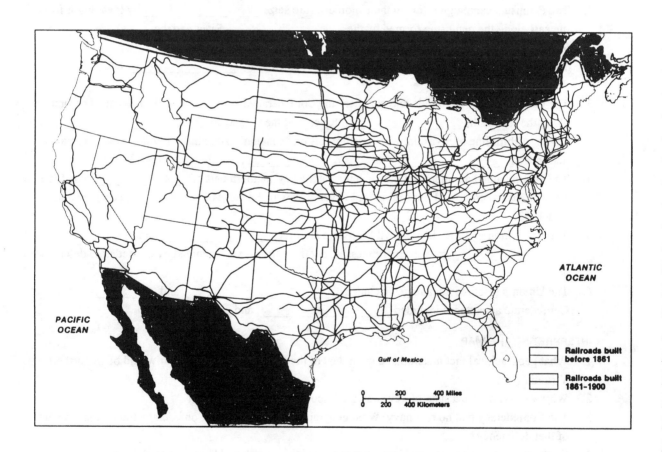

CHAPTER 2

MAPPING AMERICA

1. Railroads were the second major new transportation system to emerge in 19th-century America. The first were the canals. Label the Erie and the Main Line Canals.
2. Using a highlighter, mark some of the major railroad systems of the late nineteenth century: the Union Pacific, the Central Pacific, the Northern Pacific, and the Southern Pacific Railroads.
3. Locate with a dot, then label some of the new industrial cities that the railroads made even more dominant: San Francisco, Denver, Chicago, St. Louis, Memphis, New York, Kansas City, and Charleston.
4. Indicate on the map the locations of some of the new mining and cattle production areas in the West.

READING THE MAP

1. One of the major conflicts in the early plans for a transcontinental railroad centered on where to put the railroad's eastern terminus; in Chicago, a city in a free state, or in a slave state such as Tennessee. During the Civil War, the Union Pacific railroad was begun with its eastern terminus at _____ and its western terminus at _____.
2. The Central Pacific and the Union Pacific Railroads met up at _____, near _____ in the state of _____.
3. The _____ ran from San Francisco and Los Angeles to New Orleans and was completed in 1883.
4. The transcontinental railroads were built by immigrants from _____ and _____.

INTERPRETING THE MAP

1. What was the effect of the opening of the trans-continental railroad on the economy and society of the American West?
2. How did the railroads adapt and influence the settlement and development patterns of the United States?
3. What were the geographical factors that made a transcontinental railroad difficult to finish? What were the social and political challenges to such a project?
4. Discuss the impact of the railroad on the environment of the West.

CHAPTER 3

TERRITORIAL EXPANSION TO THE CIVIL WAR

The United States grew by gradual acquisitions of territory from which, in time, new states were organized and admitted to the Union. These acquisitions were sometimes peacefully accomplished through negotiations with Native Americans and foreign nations, but other times were the spoils of war. By the end of the Civil War, the United States was a continental republic stretching from the Atlantic to the Pacific Oceans and from Canada to Mexico and the Gulf of Mexico.

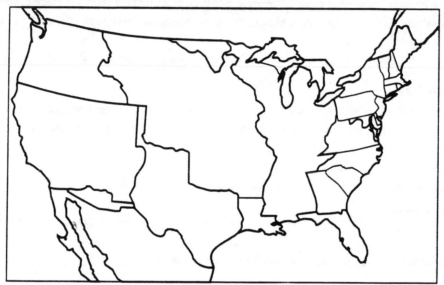

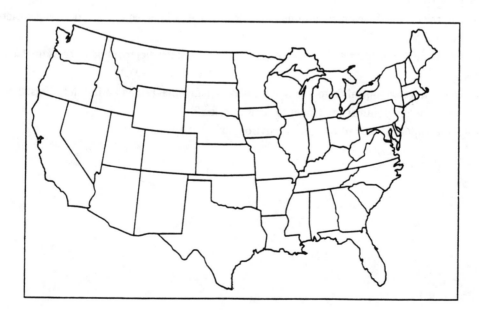

CHAPTER 3

1. Label: original thirteen states, Old Northwest, Louisiana Purchase territory, Texas, Mexican Cession territory, Oregon Country, Gadsden Purchase. Shade the territories acquired as a result of the Treaty of Paris of 1783 and the Adams-Onis Treaty (Transcontinental Treaty).

2. Mark some of the major Native American reservations in 1890, including those for the Hopi, Navajo, Ute, Apache, Crow, and Sioux.

READING THE MAP

1. List the original thirteen states. _____ _____
   _____ _____ _____ _____
   _____ _____ _____ _____
   _____ _____ _____

2. List five states whose lands include portions of the Old Northwest. _____
   _____ _____ _____ _____

3. Other than the original thirteen and those in the Old Northwest, list six states formed from territory acquired in the Treaty of Paris of 1783. _____ _____
   _____ _____ _____ _____

4. List nine states containing lands acquired in the Louisiana Purchase. _____
   _____ _____ _____ _____
   _____ _____ _____ _____

5. What state was admitted from territory acquired in the Transcontinental Treaty?
   _____

6. What state other than those of the original thirteen joined the Union without first having been a United States territory? _____

7. List three states containing lands gained in the Mexican Cession. _____
   _____ _____

8. List three states created from lands in the Oregon Country.
   _____ _____ _____

INTERPRETING THE MAP

1. In the process of transcontinental movement, Native American groups were pushed further westward. Discuss the impact of this on the development of the West.

2. Review the environmental differences and distinctions among the West, the plains states, and the eastern states. Discuss how these environmental differences might account for distinct social or political experiences. Is there a distinctive western character?

CHAPTER 4

RECONSTRUCTION

For a dozen years after the Civil War, the nation was engaged in the process of readmitting the former Confederate states into the Union. It was a slow, controversial, and, for some, painful process. Under Union aegis, the states of the Reconstruction South inaugurated Republican governments in the years immediately following the civil War. Republican power, however, was short-lived: it was not long before Southern white Democrats were able to retake state governments across the Confederacy and reassert conservative control, a process called "redemption." By the time of the Compromise of 1877, which ended Reconstruction, every Confederate state's government had been "redeemed."

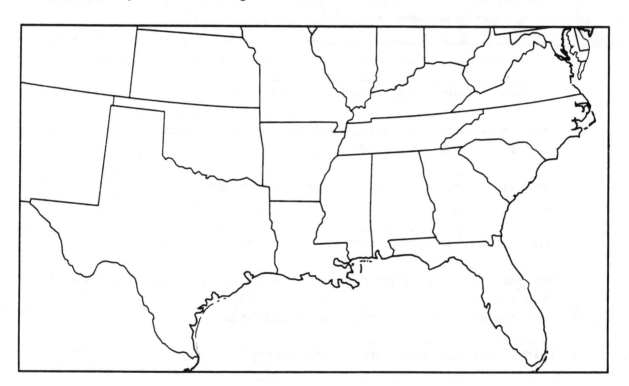

CHAPTER 4

1. Label each of the five military districts established in March 1867.
2. Indicate in each state the year that it was readmitted into the Union; also indicate the year each state was "redeemed" by conservative Democrats.

READING THE MAP

1. What was the first of the former Confederate states to be readmitted to the Union?

   _____

2. The Reconstruction Acts were passed in early 1867. Which state escaped the provisions of these laws?

   _____

3. Which two states spent the shortest time between readmission and redemption? _____

   _____

4. Which three states spent the longest time between readmission and redemption? _____

   _____ _____

5. Which state was readmitted with a conservative redeemer government already in power?

   _____

6. The Fifteenth Amendment was ratified in 1870. Which states had already been readmitted by then?

   _____ _____ _____ _____

   _____ _____ _____

7. Which three states were the last to elect redeemer governments? _____

   _____ _____

INTERPRETING THE MAP

1. In the 1867 Reconstruction Acts, why did Congress subdivide the former Confederacy geographically into five military districts?
2. What former Confederate states were most affected by the Compromise of 1877?
3. Why weren't the former Confederate states all readmitted at the same time?

CHAPTER 5

FARMERS AND THE ELECTION OF 1896

Falling prices and a growing sense of alienation from an increasingly industrial and urban society goaded American farmers to political action in the late nineteenth century. Farmers discontent crested in the free-silver crusade of William Jennings Bryan, the nominee of both the Democratic and Populist parties, in the presidential election of 1896. However, Bryan's loss of critical agricultural states that he expected to win factored heavily in his defeat by William McKinley. McKinley's victory ushered in an era of Republican dominance in national politics that would last until the Great Depression.

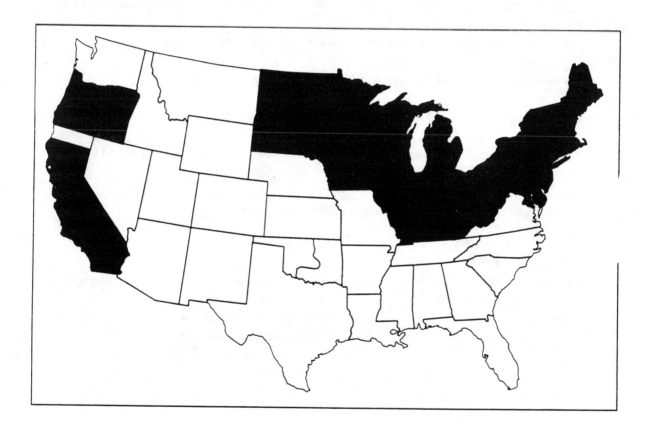

CHAPTER 5

1. Label the regions of the United States with the following abbreviations to indicate their dominant agricultural products:

    B – Beef cattle   Cn – Corn   Ct – Cotton
    D – Dairy farming   W – Wheat

2. Label the four states in which women could vote before 1900: Idaho, Utah, Wyoming, and Colorado.
3. Label: Mississippi and Ohio Rivers.
4. Indicate with a dot, then label these cities: New York, Chicago, Philadelphia, St. Louis, Boston, Baltimore, Pittsburgh, San Francisco, Cincinnati, and Cleveland.

READING THE MAP

1. What do the shaded areas on the map identify? _____
2. In 1896, which two of the following regions of the United States did McKinley win: Northeast, Midwest, Plains, South, West? _____ and _____
3. How many states did McKinley win west of the Mississippi River? _____ How many did he win south of the Ohio River–Mason-Dixon Line? _____
4. In the 1896 election, which presidential candidate, Bryan or McKinley, won the:
   cotton-producing states? _____
   beef cattle-producing states? _____
   dairy-farming states? _____
   corn-producing states? _____
   wheat-producing states? _____
5. How many states did McKinley win in 1896? _____
   How many states did Bryan win in 1896? _____
6. Which one of America's ten largest cities in 1896 was in a state won by Bryan? _____

INTERPRETING THE MAP

1. Why did the wheat- and corn-producing states in the Plains vote for Bryan, while those in the Midwest voted for McKinley?
2. What specific economic interest in the West other than the farmers gave strong support to Bryan in 1896?
3. Since there was a near equal split in the number of states won by Bryan and McKinley, how did Bryan lose so badly in the 1896 election?
4. Why did women gain the right to vote in certain western states so long before they could vote in the East?

CHAPTER 6

AMERICAN EMPIRE

Near the close of the nineteenth century, the United States reached for the first time beyond the North American continent to acquire new territory. Through both peaceful purchase and territorial conquest, the nation made its first serious bid for world-power status. Victories in the Spanish-American War and in the bloody war in the Philippines were the centerpieces of an effort to build an overseas empire, an effect driven by the desire for overseas markets and military dominance, belief in American exceptionalism, and the missionary impulse.

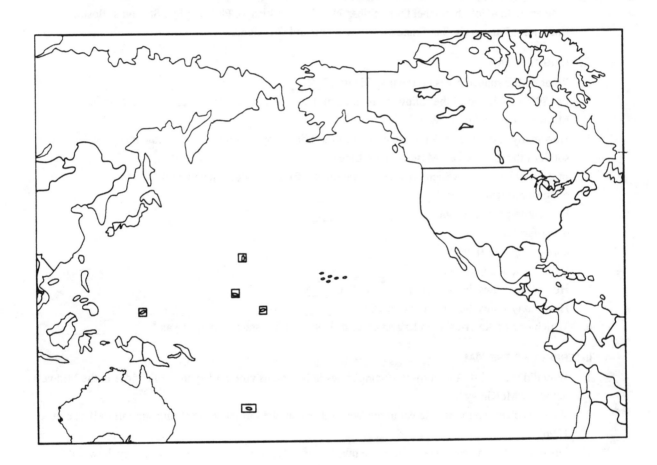

CHAPTER 6

MAPPING AMERICA

1. Label: Alaska, Cuba, Puerto Rico, British Guiana, Venezuela, Colombia, Panama, Hawaii, Midway, Wake Island, Samoa, Guam, the Philippines, China. Indicate by shading which of these were United States possessions by 1910 and write the date of acquisition under their identifying labels.
2. Indicate with a dot, then label: Manila, Guantanamo, Havana.
3. Label: Caribbean Sea, Gulf of Mexico, South China Sea, Pacific Ocean.

READING THE MAP

1. By 1910, what United States possession was most distant from the continental United States? _____ What was the United States's nearest possession? _____
2. Most American overseas possessions by 1910 were acquired during the Spanish-American War or in the peace treaty that ended it. What two territories were acquired *before* the war?

   _____ _____
3. The dispute that involved the United States in a controversy with Britain in 1893 concerned the boundary between two nations in (select one): Central America, South America, the Caribbean?

   _____
4. The only United States possession by 1910 that was not an island, part of an island, or a set of islands was _____.
5. In the Treaty of Paris in 1898 the United States acquired two territories in the Pacific and one in the Caribbean. Those in the Pacific were _____ and _____, and that in the Caribbean was _____.

INTERPRETING THE MAP

1. Cuba is less than 100 miles from the United States. The Philippines are thousands of miles away. Given this, why did the Spanish-American War begin with a U.S. naval attack in the Philippines?
2. It took about eight weeks for the United States to win the Spanish-American War. It took nearly four years to win the war in the Philippines. What geographical circumstances help explain this difference?
3. When Secretary of State Seward recommended the purchase of Alaska in 1867, critics referred to it as "Seward's folly" and wondered why over $7 million was spent on this "icebox." What geographical and strategic considerations could Seward have had in mind when he made the purchase?

CHAPTER 7

THE UNITED STATES IN ASIA, 1900–1940

The United States had a long-standing interest in China and Asia that was fueled by American business's hunger to open the Far East to investment and trade as well as American religious missionaries proselytization activities. Yet at the same time, turn-of-the-century Americans continued to exhibit strong racial prejudice toward Asian immigrants especially on the West Coast, and such prejudice was evident in American immigration policies of the era. The Japanese in particular resented these racist policies and the open discrimination against Japanese immigrants on the West Coast. And so Japan grew stronger in Asia, relations between it and the United States grew increasingly strained.

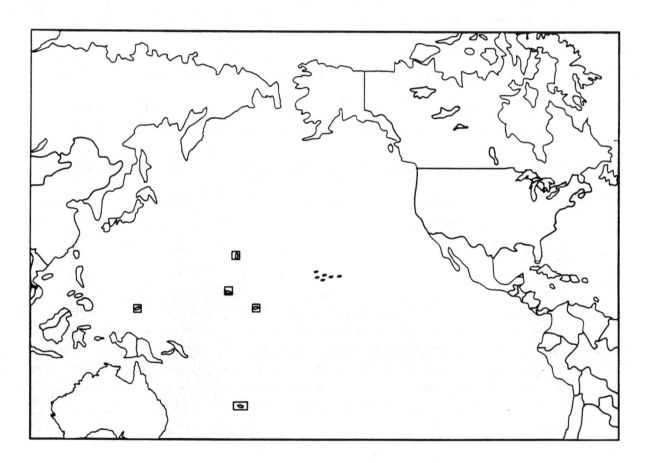

CHAPTER 7

1. Label: Russia, Manchuria, China, Japan, Sea of Japan, Korea, Philippine Islands, Guam, Wake, Midway, Hawaii, Pacific Ocean, United States, Alaska.

READING THE MAP

1. In 1910, the American possession lying closest to the Asian mainland was _____ .
2. In 1910, the American possession lying closest to China was _____ .
3. Between mainland United States and the Philippine Islands the United States possessed several Pacific Islands by 1910. The three American island possessions lying most directly on a line from the continental United States to the Philippines were _____ , _____ and _____ .
4. The Philippines and Japan are island nations, both about equidistant from the coast of what Asian mainland nation? _____
5. What Asian peninsular nation lies just across the Sea of Japan from Japan? _____
6. Manchuria is bordered on the north and east by _____ , on the west by _____ , and on the south by _____ .

INTERPRETING THE MAP

1. After over a hundred years of isolation from Asia, why did the United States become involved in that area of the world at the beginning of the twentieth century?
2. What territorial arrangements did the United States make with Japan in the Far East between 1900 and 1940?
3. Why was Japan territorially ambitious in the 1930s, and what was the United States' response to that ambition?

CHAPTER 8

THE UNITED STATES IN LATIN AMERICA, 1900–1930

Between 1900 and 1930, the United States established a well-protected sphere of influence in Central America and the Caribbean. The Caribbean Sea became a virtual American lake over which the United States exercised an international police power. Justified by the 1904 Roosevelt Corollary to the Monroe Doctrine, the United States risked the resentment of all Latin America by adopting an interventionist foreign policy that threatened the sovereignty of Central American and Caribbean nations.

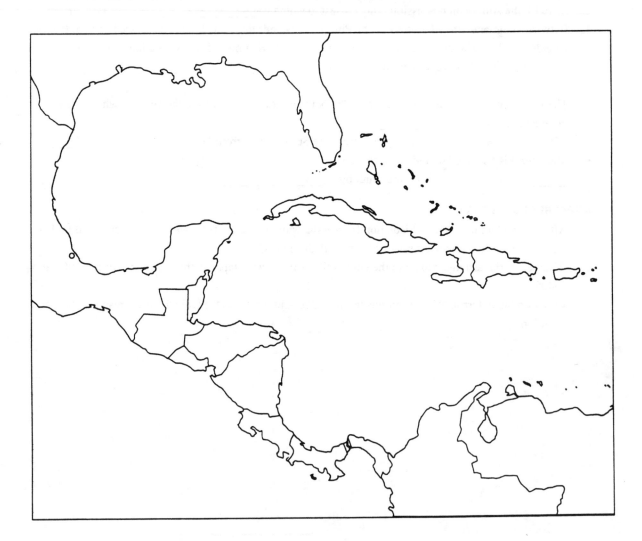

CHAPTER 8

MAPPING AMERICA

1. Label: Gulf of Mexico, Caribbean Sea, Guantanamo Bay, Atlantic Ocean, Pacific Ocean.
2. Label: Puerto Rico, Dominican Republic, Haiti, Cuba, Mexico, British Honduras, Honduras, El Salvador, Nicaragua, Costa Rica, Panama, Canal Zone, Colombia, Venezuela.
3. Shade the territories the United States annexed, purchased, or leased in Central America and the Caribbean to 1930. Write in the acquisition dates of these territories.

READING THE MAP

1. What territories in Central America and the Caribbean did the United States acquire or lease
   by 1900? _____
   by 1910? _____
   by 1920? _____
2. The Gulf of Mexico is bounded by the coastlines of what three countries? _____
   _____ _____
3. a. Name three countries that border the Caribbean Sea on the west.

   _____ _____ _____

   b. Name three countries that border the Caribbean Sea on the south.

   _____ _____ _____

   c. Name three countries that border the Caribbean Sea on the north.

   _____ _____ _____
4. The Caribbean island that is closest to the United States is _____.
5. The Canal Zone is a water passage between which two bodies of water? _____ and

   _____

INTERPRETING THE MAP

1. In the territorial settlement that ended the Spanish-American War, the United States annexed the Philippine Islands and Puerto Rico. Since American armies occupied Cuba when the war ended, why wasn't Cuba annexed as well?
2. There was a controversy about where to construct an isthmian canal through Central America. What geographical considerations led to the selection of Panama for the canal route?
3. At present the United States still operates a naval base at Guantanamo Bay, Cuba. How did the United States get possession of this territory?
4. Discuss the reasons for American intervention in Central America and the Caribbean. What were the environmental and strategic features of this area that American policymakers were so interested in?
5. Investigate the agriculture of Central America and the Caribbean and locate on the map the major areas of American investment. Map out major inter-American trade routes. Discuss the effect these may have had on American intervention in the region.

CHAPTER 9

IMMIGRATION, 1870–1930

The United States is a nation of immigrants. Immigrants from all over the world have continuously added to America's population growth and its ethnic and cultural diversity. There was an especially heavy volume of European immigration to America in the half century between 1870 and 1920. these immigrants came from different places than did earlier immigrants, and in larger numbers. They helped settle a new environment: a dynamic and urban industrial America.

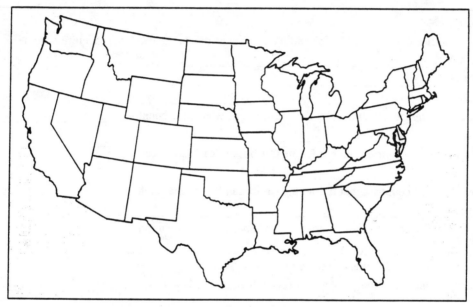

CHAPTER 9

1. Label: Britain, Ireland, Norway, Sweden, Germany, Italy, Russia, Greece.
2. Indicate with a dot, then label the ten largest cities in America in 1910: New York City, Philadelphia, Boston, Chicago, Cleveland, Pittsburgh, Buffalo, St. Louis, Baltimore, Detroit.
3. Draw a boundary that encompasses all these "big city" dots and label this the core "urban zone" in America in 1910.
4. Use different shadings to indicate, then label: (1) northern and western Europe, (2) southern and eastern Europe.

READING THE MAP

1. Three nations that were sources of the "old" immigration were _____, _____, and _____.
2. Three nations that were sources of the "new" immigration were _____, _____, and _____.
3. In 1870, 1880, and 1890, most immigrants to the United States came from what area of Europe? _____ In 1900, most came from what areas? _____
4. From which areas of Europe did the number of immigrants to America steadily increase between 1870 and 1900? _____
5. The peak year of immigration to the United States between 1870 and 1900 was _____. The most dramatic *decrease* of annual immigration to the United States between 1870 and 1920 began in the year _____.
6. The geographical preference of "new" immigrants coming to America was to settle in (select one): big cities, small towns, the South, the Plains states. _____
7. One major source nation for Asian immigration to America between 1870 and 1900 was _____.

INTERPRETING THE MAP

1. What environmental considerations help explain the enormous increase in the volume of immigration to America between 1870 and 1920?
2. The destination of most "new" immigrants to America was different than most "old" immigrants. Where was it and why did "new" immigrants tend to move there?
3. The source area of the "new" immigrants was different from that of the "old" immigrants. Where did the "new" immigrants come from and why did the source area shift?

CHAPTER 10

THE UNITED STATES IN WORLD WAR I

World War I—The Great War–began in Europe in 1914. For three years the United States struggled to maintain its neutrality, but in 1917, compelling circumstances drew the United States into the conflict. For the first time in the nation's history, American troops fought in Europe, and their presence proved decisive on the western front. Because they entered the war to help "make the world safe for democracy," Americans were exultant in victory, and in its aftermath they looked forward to shaping a new, peaceful world free of the nationalistic interests and feuds of previous centuries.

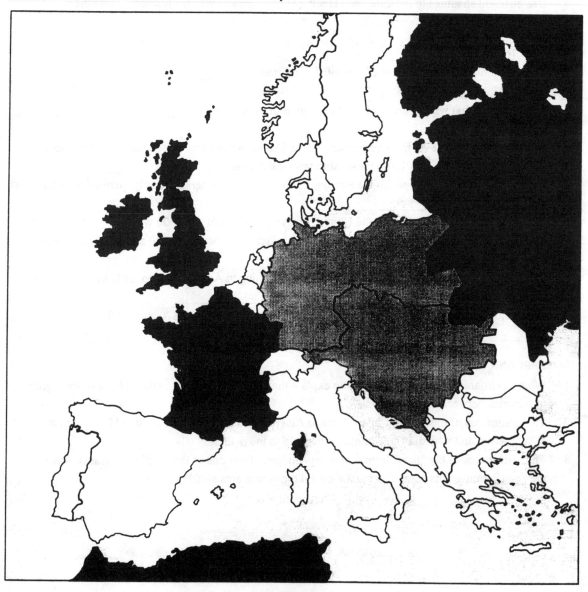

CHAPTER 10

1. Label: Great Britain, English Channel, North Sea, France, Germany, Italy, Austria-Hungary, Switzerland, Russia, Serbia.
2. Label: (1) the Central Powers (Triple Alliance) and (2) the Allied Powers (Triple Entente) at the beginning of World War I.
3. Use an X to locate, then label these battles: Château-Thierry, Belleau Wood, Cantigny, St. Mihiel, Verdun, Meuse-Argonne.
4. Draw a bold line to identify the western front in World War I.

READING THE MAP

1. Two nations among the Central Powers when World War I began were _____ and
   _____.
2. Three nations among the Allied Powers when World War I began were _____,
   _____, and _____.
3. Which nation had to fight a two front war on its own borders in World War I? _____
4. The major battles in which American troops participated in World War I were all in what country?
   _____
5. In order to inhibit shipping into German ports, the Allies could best mine and patrol what body of water? _____
6. Where could the Germans best position their submarines to inhibit the American shipping Allies?
   _____

INTERPRETING THE MAP

1. What fact of geography kept Americans from expressing a sense of urgency for their nation's national security when war broke out in Europe in 1914?
2. What were the geographical characteristics of the western front in World War I?
3. What were the geographical implications of the notorious Zimmermann telegram in 1917?

CHAPTER 11

AFRICAN AMERICAN MIGRATION

Beginning immediately after the Civil War and continuing into the middle of the twentieth century, African Americans migrated from the rural South to Northern cities. Almost one million African Americans left the South between 1897 and 1900; some 85 percent of them settled in the industrial cities of the North. During World War I the flow of African Americans north intensified, as conditions in the South worsened and jobs seemed even more available in the North. Half a million African Americans went North in 1918 as part of what became known as the Great Exodus. The journey, however, was far from east —white southerners, fearful of losing cheap agricultural labor, often tried to prevent black from leaving by attacking the trains they rode on, while in the North, blacks were frequently met with violence from whites who saw them as threats to their own jobs. In addition, though perhaps it was not codified in law as in the South, there was pervasive racism in the North as well. African Americans faced fierce discrimination as they sought jobs in factories and many were forced to take the very lowest-paying jobs.

CHAPTER 11

MAPPING AMERICA

1. Label: Washington, D.C., Tuskegee, Alabama, Atlanta, Harlem, Chicago, Detroit, East St. Louis.
2. Draw the route of the Illinois Central Railroad which ran between New Orleans and Chicago.
3. Draw the route of the Southern Railroad, which linked New Orleans, Birmingham, Atlanta, Charlottesville, and Washington, D.C.

READING THE MAP

1. The eastern city of _____ was a major gateway for the movement from the South to the North.
2. Note the interesting movement southward as blacks from South Carolina and Georgia relocated in

   _____.
3. Most African Americans went north on the _____.
4. There were *major* race riots after World War I in the cities of _____.

INTERPRETING THE MAP

1. What were the causes of the Great Migration? Why did it intensify around World War I?
2. What was the impact of the Great Migration on the southern economy? On the northern cities?

CHAPTER 12

EUROPE BETWEEN THE WARS

At the end of World War I, the delegates at the peace conference in Versailles redrew the map of Europe. Some nations lost territory, some disappeared entirely. Some nations gained territory, some were created anew. This new quilt of national boundaries was delicate; few nations were fully satisfied with the borders given them in 1919, and an intense spirit of ethnic nationalism continuously jeopardized national stability. By 1939 all these borders were imperiled again, and again it was an expansionist Germany that posed the threat.

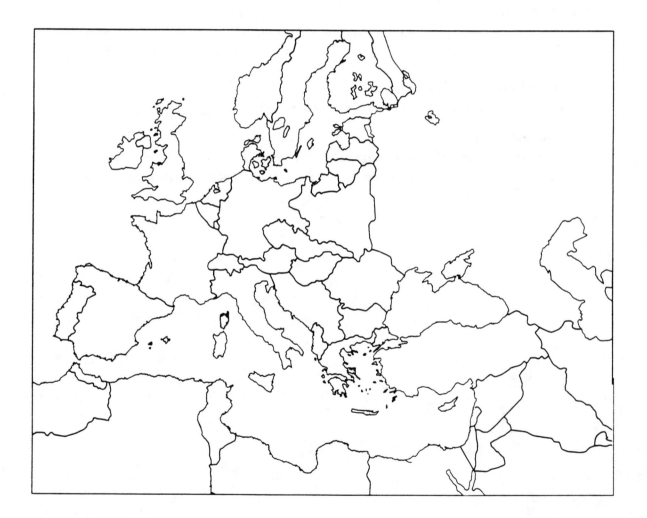

CHAPTER 12

1. Label: Great Britain, Ireland (Irish Free State), Portugal, Spain, France, Belgium, Netherlands, Luxembourg, Italy, Germany, Switzerland, Austria, Hungary, Czechoslovakia, Poland, East Prussia, Yugoslavia, Rumania, Lithuania, Latvia, Estonia, Denmark, Finland, Sweden, Norway, Soviet Union.
2. Label: Atlantic Ocean, English Channel, North Sea, Baltic Sea, Black Sea, Mediterranean Sea,.
3. Consult a historical atlas, then draw in, shadow, and label: Saar Basin, Sudetenland, Alsace-Lorraine, Rhineland, Polish Corridor, Danzig (Gdansk).
4. Circle the names of the *new* nations created in 1919.

READING THE MAP

1. Name three European nations that were created in 1919._____ _____
   _____
2. Name two existing nations whose territory expanded in 1919._____
   _____
3. Name three existing nations that lost territory in 1919. _____ _____
   _____
4. Name two nations in addition to Austria and Hungary that were created from the prewar empire of Austria-Hungary. _____ _____
5. Name two nations that disappeared in the creation of Yugoslavia. _____
   _____
6. Which nation lost its ports on the Baltic Sea in 1919? _____
7. Name three nations to whom Germany transferred territory in 1919. _____
   _____ _____
8. What nation was formed out of territory taken from Germany, the Soviet Union, and Austria-Hungary in 1919? _____

INTERPRETING THE MAP

1. Speculate on why, in the Versailles treaty, Germany proper was separated from East Prussia (part of Germany) by a slender piece of territory given to Poland.
2. Note the location of the new nations created in 1919. With what nation do several of them share boundary? What might this suggest about the rationale for their creation?
3. What criterion figured heavily in the Versailles Conference's redrawing of the boundaries of Europe in 1919?

CHAPTER 13

NEW CONSUMERISM AND GENDER ROLES IN THE 1920S: A SEARS HOUSE

The 1920s were a decade of great social change in America. More women than ever before were venturing outside the home into the workforce and the popularization of birth control altered gender roles. Meanwhile a prosperous American economy placed an ever-increasing array of consumer goods, like the automobile, within the reach of more Americans. One of the more interesting mass-consumer goods to emerge during the period was the Sears House, a moderately priced model home that allowed many working-class people to purchase their own homes for the first time. Called a "bungalow," after the houses in British India it was designed after, it was popular from about 1910 until 1930, and its plan revealed much about the values of its era.

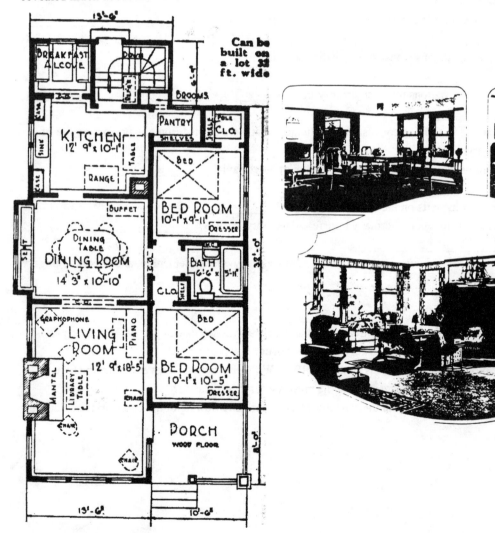

CHAPTER 13

MAPPING AMERICA

1. Label the areas in the public and private areas of the house.

READING THE MAP

1. Access to this house was _____, in that one could not see the front door from the street and it was obscured by the front porch.
2. This house was designed for a culture built around _____ rather than the automobile.

INTERPRETING THE MAP

1. What new technology is incorporated into the Sears House that reflects the 1920's culture of consumption? What impact did that technology have on everyday life?
2. What is different about this living space from that of lower- and middle-class Americans living in cities?
3. What new standards of living are illustrated in this floor plan?
4. How might women's lives have been particularly affected by moving into a Sears House?
5. How many children would fit into this Sears House? What does this say about the impact of family planning and the changed expectations Americans brought to married life?

CHAPTER 14

WORLD WAR II IN EUROPE AND NORTH AFRICA

Just days after the Japanese attack on the American Pacific Fleet at Pearl Harbor on December 7, 1941, Germany as well declared war on the United States. Thus the United States was drawn in to World War II. In the European theater, the United States and its allies, the Grand Alliance, fought Japan's partners in the Axis, Germany and Italy. Fighting raged across the Continent from England to Russia and from Norway to North Africa for three and a half years until the Allies finally prevailed on May 8, 1945, V-E (Victory in Europe) Day.

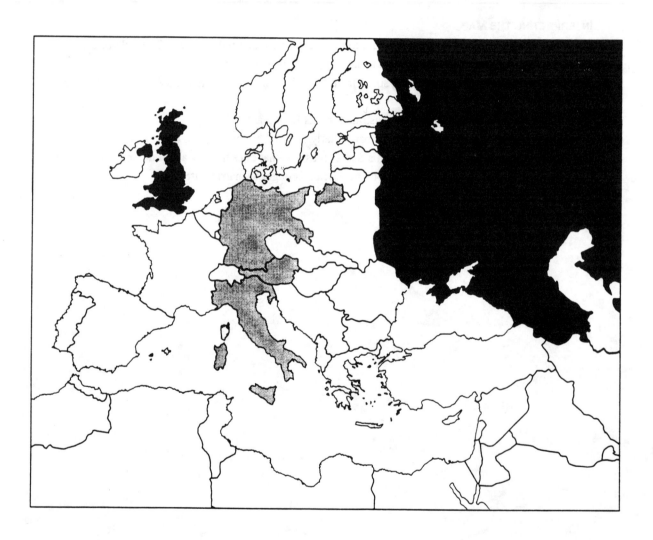

CHAPTER 14

1. Label: Great Britain, Ireland, France, Portugal, Spain, Italy, Egypt, Switzerland, Norway, Sweden,. Germany, Soviet Union,

2. Indicate with a dot, then label: Caen, Cherbourg, Rome, Berlin, Potsdam, Moscow, Stalingrad, Yalta, Cairo, El Alamein, Teheran, Casablanca.

3. Label: Normandy coast, English Channel, North Sea, Black Sea, Mediterranean Sea, Suez Canal, Sicily.

4. Label: (1) the Axis Powers, and (2) the Allied Powers in Europe in World War II.

READING THE MAP

1. What were the two major Axis Powers in Europe in World War II? _____
   _____

2. What were the two major Allied Powers in Europe in World War II? _____
   _____

3. What were three neutral nations in Europe in World War II? _____
   _____ _____

4. What body of water did the "second front" Allied invasion force cross on June 6, 1944?
   _____ On what coast did it land? _____

5. In what country did the key battle of El Alamein occur? _____

6. There were several major wartime conferences before Potsdam in 1945. Where were three of these conferences held? _____ _____ _____

7. The furthest penetration of German armies into the Soviet Union was stopped at the crucial battle for what city? _____

INTERPRETING THE MAP

1. What geographical advantage was there to the Allied strategy designed to drive the Germans from North Africa *before* invading Axis-held Europe?

2. What considerations made the battle of Stalingrad the turning point of World War II in Europe?

3. What helped determine the landing site for opening the Allies' "second front" in Europe?

CHAPTER 15

WORLD WAR II IN THE PACIFIC

After Japan's surprise attack on Pearl Harbor and the subsequent German declaration of war, the United States decided to concentrate its efforts in Europe and fought a holding action against the Japanese in the Pacific. Successes in Europe in 1943 allowed the United States to place more men and matériel in the Pacific theater. Skillful naval warfare in tandem with a methodical "island hopping" campaign brought the United States within striking distance of the Japanese home islands by the summer of 1945.

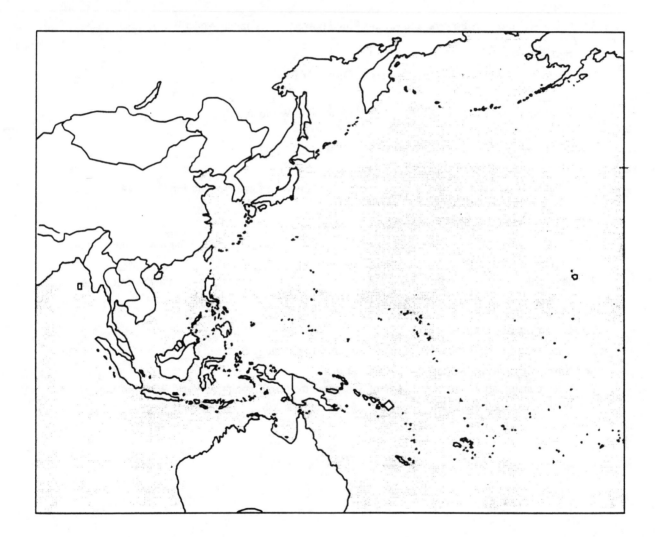

CHAPTER 15

1. Label: Japan, Korea, Manchuria, China, Philippines, Malaya, Burma, French Indochina, Australia, Netherlands (Dutch), East Indies.
2. Label: Aleutian Islands, Midway, Wake Island, Guam, Iwo Jima, Saipan, Okinawa, New Guinea, Marshall Islands, Solomon Islands, Gilbert Islands, Guadalcanal.
3. Label: Coral Sea, Pacific Ocean, Indian Ocean.
4. Indicate with a dot, then label: Pearl Harbor, Tokyo, Hiroshima, Nagasaki.
5. Draw a line indicating the furthest extent of Japanese control in Asia and the Pacific during World War II.

READING THE MAP

1. What were three countries on the Asian mainland Japan controlled during World War II?
   _____ _____ _____
2. What three large island groups did Japan control during World War II? _____
   _____ _____
3. The westernmost attack by Japanese forces in the Pacific came on the _____ Islands.
4. At its furthest extent, the Japanese Empire controlled territory as far north as the _____
   Islands, as far east as the _____ Islands, and as far south as the _____
   Islands.
5. By mid-1945 the islands closest to Japan that were held by the United States were _____
   and _____.
6. American victories at Guadalcanal and the Coral Sea were important in that they protected United States supply and communication lines leading to _____.
7. America's two-pronged advance across the Pacific was aimed at liberating what former United States possession that had been captured earlier by Japan? _____

INTERPRETING THE MAP

1. What effect did the geographical factor of distance have on America's conduct of military operations in the Pacific theater during World War II?
2. What is the key importance of the geographical position of the Philippine Islands for the balance of power in the Far Pacific during World War II?
3. What geographical features of Iwo Jima made it the scene of one of the bloodiest campaigns of World War II?
4. Consider the strategic gains—in access to raw materials, overcoming geographical obstacles, and increased technological capabilities—the Allies made as they pursued Japan.

CHAPTER 16

THE COLD WAR IN EUROPE

As World War II ended in 1945, the Grand Alliance broke up. The former wartime allies fell into a "Cold War"— an ideological struggle for control of territory and political influence that seldom escalated to direct confrontation, but instead was conducted by diplomatic subterfuges, political and military brinkmanship, and using weaker "satellite" nations as pawns and intermediaries. The contest began over questions related to eastern Europe, but came eventually to involve competition between the postwar superpowers, the United States and the Soviet Union, throughout the world. The United States, pursuing a "containment" policy against the Soviet Union, remilitarized, formed alliances, and brandished its nuclear weaponry in a frustrating attempt to counter the threat it saw in Soviet expansion.

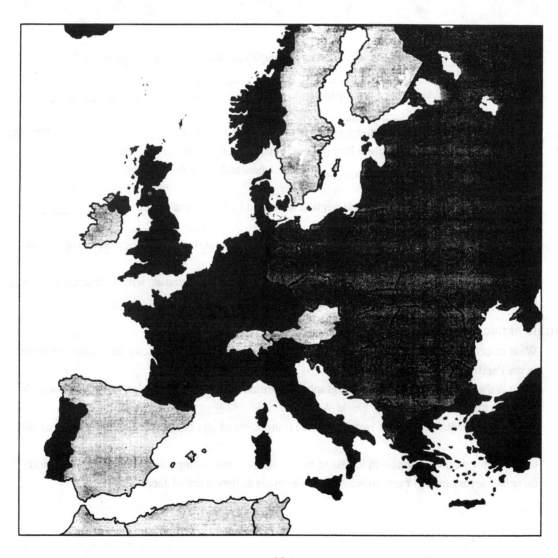

CHAPTER 16

MAPPING AMERICA

1. Label: Norway, Sweden, Finland, Great Britain, Ireland, Spain, France, Luxembourg, Belgium, West Germany, East Germany, Switzerland, Austria, Italy, Czechoslovakia, Poland, Bulgaria, Soviet Union, Hungary, Yugoslavia, Rumania, Albania, Turkey, Greece.
2. Label: Bosporus and Dardanelles straits, Black Sea, Aegean Sea, Mediterranean Sea, Adriatic Sea, Baltic Sea.
3. Label: Western bloc nations and Communist bloc nations in postwar Europe.
4. Use a dot to locate, then label: Vienna, Berlin, Trieste, Stettin (Szezecin), Prague, Sofia, Budapest, Bucharest, Belgrade.
5. Use a bold line to draw the boundaries of the "iron curtain" defined by Winston Churchill in 1946.

READING THE MAP

1. Name three East European nations that were occupied by the Soviet Union at the end of World War II.

    _____ _____ _____
2. The first Cold War clash between the United States and the Soviet Union came over the kind of government to be established in what Eastern European nation? _____
3. The Truman Doctrine implemented the containment doctrine regarding what two countries?

    _____ _____
4. The threat of the growing strength of the communist parties in what two Western European countries provoked the Marshall Plan? _____ _____
5. In 1948, President Truman ordered an airlift to counter the Soviet move to blockade what city?

    _____
6. What Eastern European country was the scene of a bloody revolt against Soviet dominance in 1956?

    _____
7. Which former Axis power was geographically divided between members of the Grand Alliance at the end of World War II? _____

INTERPRETING THE MAP

1. What major decisions were reached at the Yalta Conference that changed the post-war map of Europe?
2. How did Eastern Europe come to be dominated by the Soviet Union at the end of World War II?
3. What geographical consideration made Greece and Turkey important to the containment policy against Soviet expansion?

CHAPTER 17

THE KOREAN WAR AND THE COLD WAR IN ASIA

In 1945 the United States occupied a defeated Japan, thereby expanding America's role as an Asian power. The fall of China to Communist revolutionaries in 1949 was a blow to United States interests in Asia, but did not provoke a military response. The North Korean invasion of South Korea in June, 1950, did. United States troops participated in a United Nations "police action" to contain communism in Korea, but, with China threatening to enter the fray on the side of North Korea, the effort stalemated in 1953. Not until 1979 did the United States formally recognize the Communist government of China, and Korea is still divided along the demilitarized zone agreed to in 1953.

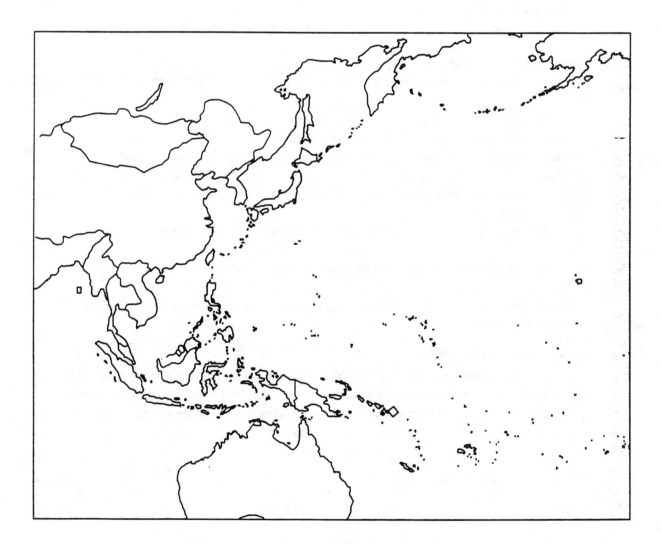

CHAPTER 17

MAPPING AMERICA

1. Label: People's Republic of China, Formosa (Taiwan), the Philippines, Japan, Siberia.
2. Indicate with a dot, then label: Peking (Beijing), Seoul, Panmunjon, Pusan, Inchon.
3. Draw a line along the 38th parallel (38° N latitude).
4. Label: Yalu River, Sea of Japan, Yellow Sea.

READING THE MAP

1. In 1949 Maoist revolutionaries established a Communist government in mainland
   _____ with its capital in the city of _____ .
2. In 1949, the United States supported the Nationalist government of China, which fled to the island of
   _____ . The island was renamed _____ .
3. What nations border Korea on the north? _____ _____ To the east, just
   across the Sea of Japan is _____ .
4. Within days after invading, North Korean troops had pushed South Korean defenses southward to a
   small defense perimeter around the city of _____ .
5. When United Nations troops came to the aid of South Korea in 1950, General Douglas MacArthur
   devised an ingenious and brilliantly executed behind-the-lines landing at _____ that
   nearly trapped the North Koreans.
6. President Truman temporarily abandoned the United State's containment policy when he ordered U.N.
   troops to cross the _____ and "liberate" North Korea.
7. Communist Chinese troops entered the Korean War when U.N. troops moved close to the North
   Korean–Chinese border along the _____ River .

INTERPRETING THE MAP

1. South Korea was not an American possession, nor even defined within the American defense
   perimeter, so why did President Truman send American troops to defend South Korea?
2. What territorial ambitions did the United States have in Asia in the 1940s and 1950s?
3. What geographical features of the Korean peninsula complicated military action during the Korean
   War?

CHAPTER 18

POPULATION MOBILITY IN THE TWENTIETH CENTURY

Americans have always been mobile. Historically, population movement and an itching restlessness has been one of the defining characteristics of the American people. Post-World War II Americans sustained that tradition, propelled by a rising birth rate, renewed foreign immigration, and the incessant quest for economic opportunity. These contributed to burgeoning population growth in some cities and regions of the country and the decline of others.

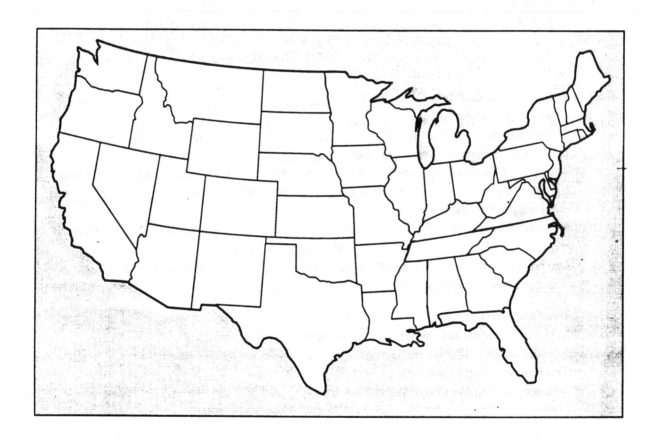

CHAPTER 18

1. Indicate with a dot, then label: Tucson, San Diego, Phoenix, Atlanta, New Orleans, Dallas, Los Angeles, San Antonio, Miami, Houston.
2. Use a variety of shadings to show those states with:
   - the highest percentage population increase, 1940–1950.
   - the highest percentage population increase, 1980–1990.
   - the lowest percentage population increase, 1940–1950.
   - the lowest percentage population increase, 1980–1990.
   - a population decline, 1940–1950.
   - a population decline, 1980–1990.

READING THE MAP

1. Which region of the country had the slowest population growth, 1940–1950? _____
   Which regions had the slowest population growth, 1980-1990? _____

   _____ _____
2. In what direction did the population generally move in both 1940–1950 and in 1980–1990?

   _____
3. Of those you have located, which city had the largest absolute population increase, 1940–1960?
   _____ 1960–1980? _____
4. What three eastern states with a high percentage population increase in 1940–1950 did *not* fit this category in 1980–1990? _____ _____ _____
5. Name three states whose population was increasing in 1940–1950, but whose population was declining in 1980–1990. _____ _____ _____
6. What was a western state that lost population in 1980–1990? _____
7. What two regions of the country had a moderate to high population increase in 1940-1950, but a low increase or decline of population in 1980–1990? _____ _____

INTERPRETING THE MAP

1. Discuss the environmental and technological changes which made the major population shifts of the 1970s and 1980s possible.
2. Discuss how federal spending may have fostered these population shifts.
3. How have these population shifts affected party politics and political power?

CHAPTER 19

THE VIETNAM WAR

The United States fought its longest and least successful war in Vietnam. American strategy was to fight a limited war in South Vietnam to contain communism, while the Vietcong and North Vietnamese fought a protracted, succeeded in total war for national unification and liberation. In 1975, just over two years after the United States had ended its military involvement in Vietnam, a North Vietnamese invasion of the South succeeded in unifying Vietnam under a Communist government.

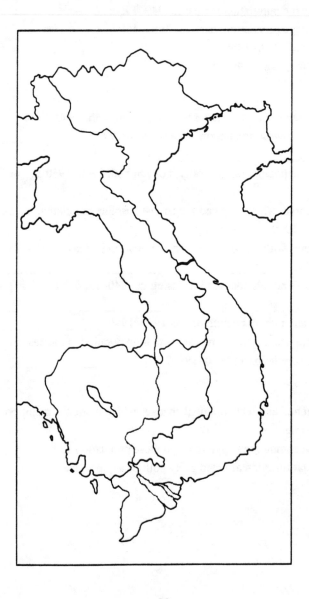

CHAPTER 19

1. Label: North Vietnam, South Vietnam, Cambodia, Laos, China, Thailand.
2. Indicate with a dot, then label: Dien Bien Phu, Haiphong, Hanoi, Hue, My Lai, Pleiku, Saigon, Da Nang, Khe Sanh.
3. Label: Mekong River, Gulf of Tonkin, Cam Ranh Bay, South China Sea.
4. Draw a bold line to trace the route of the Ho Chi Minh Trail. Draw a light line along 17° N latitude. Draw a circle around the DMZ (Demilitarized Zone).

READING THE MAP

1. In addition to the other, North Vietnam bordered both _____ and _____, and South Vietnam bordered both _____ and _____.
2. The Mekong River forms a portion of the western boundary of _____ and ultimately drains into the _____.
3. Dien Bien Phu, where French forces were defeated by Ho Chi Minh's army in 1954, was located in northwest _____ near its border with _____.
4. Former French Indochina was divided into North and South Vietnam by a narrow _____ that lay generally along the _____ parallel.
5. The 1964 incident that resulted in a war resolution from the United States. Congress allegedly occurred in the _____ just off the coast of _____.
6. The Ho Chi Minh Trail ran from North Vietnam through _____ and _____ into South Vietnam.

INTERPRETING THE MAP

1. Why did the location of Vietnam seem strategically important enough for the United States to commit so deeply to its defense?
2. What geographical conditions in Vietnam influenced the conduct of military operations there?
3. How did Vietnam first come to be geographically divided into two parts, North and South Vietnam?

CHAPTER 20

IMMIGRATION, 1950–1990

Immigration has continued to be a major theme in post-World War II America. Thousands of people still come to the United States every year from all parts of the world seeking, among other things, the promise of economic opportunity—the same motive that has brought so many millions to these shores since the founding of Jamestown in 1607. Yet, in postwar America, some new subthemes have emerged as U.S. immigration law has changed and key world events have played a role in changing the patterns of American immigration.

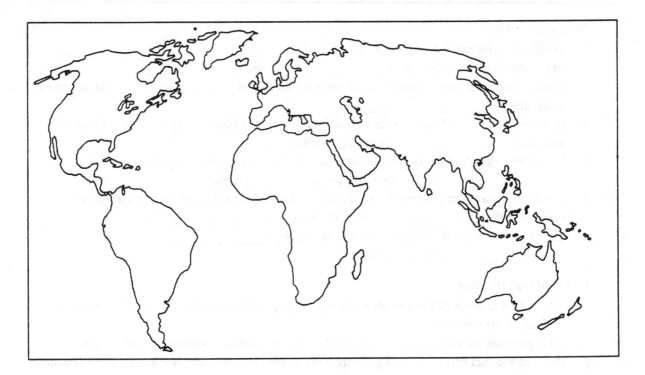

CHAPTER 20

MAPPING AMERICA

1. Draw an approximate boundary around, then label each of the following: Latin America, northwestern Europe, southeastern Europe, Asia.
2. In each of the areas, write in the approximate number of immigrants (within 50,000) from that area to the United States in each of the following decades. Use this key:
   a. 1951–1960
   b. 1961–1970
   c. 1971–1980
   d. 1981–1989

READING THE MAP

1. What area outside of North America contributed the *most* immigrants to the United States in the 1950s?_____ in the 1960s?_____ in the 1970s? _____ in the 1980s? _____
2. What area outside of North America contributed the *fewest* immigrants to the United States in the 1950s? _____ in the 1960s?_____ in the 1970s? _____ in the 1980s? _____
3. Which area had the largest increase in the number of immigrants sent to the United States from the 1950s to the 1960s? _____ From the 1960s to the 1970s? _____ From the 1970s to the 1980s? _____
4. Which area sent the *largest* total number of immigrants to the United States between 1951 and 1989? _____ Which area sent the *smallest* total number? _____
5. What two areas show a steady decade-by-decade increase between 1950 and 1989 in the total number of immigrants sent to the United States? _____ and _____
6. What area shows a steady decade-by-decade decrease between 1950 and 1989 in the total number of immigrants sent to the United States? _____

INTERPRETING THE MAP

1. What historical events have helped shape the flow of immigration from Europe since World War II?
2. What historical events have helped shape the flow of immigration from Latin America since World War II?
3. What historical events have helped shape the flow of immigration from Asia since World War II?

CHAPTER 21

THE UNITED STATES AND THE MIDDLE EAST

In addition to being the world's foremost source of oil, the Middle East is one the most strategically located areas in the world as it connects Africa, Europe and Asia. It is also one of the most unstable. The area was a theater of East-West conflict in the Cold War after World War II, and both the Western and Communist blocs had vital interests there. But since even before World War II, the Middle East had a long history of violent territorial and religious-ethnic conflict. The area's problems often seem irresolvable.

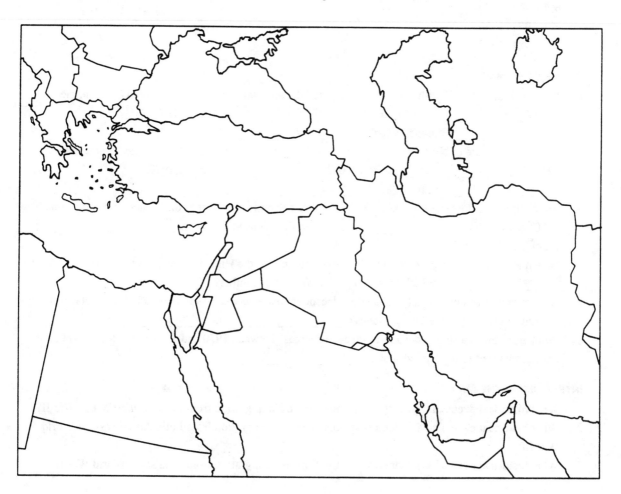

CHAPTER 21

MAPPING AMERICA

1. Label: Turkey, Cyprus, Egypt, Israel, Lebanon, Jordan, Syria, Saudi Arabia, Kuwait, Iraq, Iran, Commonwealth of Independent States (CIS), Afghanistan.
2. Label: Black Sea, Caspian Sea, Dardanelles, Bosporus Straits, Mediterranean Sea, Jordan River, Suez Canal, Red Sea, Gulf of Oman, Persian Gulf, Strait of Hormuz.
3. Label: Gaza Strip, Sinai Peninsula, West Bank, Golan Heights.
4. Locate with a dot, then label: Beirut, Jerusalem, Tel Aviv, Baghdad, Teheran.

READING THE MAP

1. The Suez Canal is a water passage connecting the _____ and _____.
2. What nations in the Middle East are entirely land locked? _____
3. What is the largest nation in the Middle East? _____
4. In the north, Iran is bordered by _____; in the south, it is bordered by

    _____ .
5. What three large nations border the Persian Gulf? _____ _____

    _____
6. What four nations border Israel? _____ _____ _____

    _____
7. The West Bank area is on the western bank of what river? _____
8. The Strait of Hormuz links what two bodies of water? _____ _____
9. What nation was involved in wars with Iran from 1980–1988 and with U.N. coalition forces in 1991?

    _____

INTERPRETING THE MAP

1. The modern nation of Israel does not appear on maps that predate World War II. Why not?
2. How does its location help explain why the Middle East plays a major role in American foreign policy and international diplomacy?
3. What geographical conditions contributed to the success of U.N. forces in the Persian Gulf War?

CHAPTER 22

THE UNITED STATES, CENTRAL AMERICA, AND THE CARIBBEAN

Central America and the Caribbean have had a special importance to the United States dating back to the Monroe Doctrine in 1823. American security and economic interests have kept the United States actively involved in the region's affairs throughout the twentieth century. Disorder and instability in area has often provoked U.S. intervention, exacerbating a troubled relationship already characterized by mistrust and resentment.

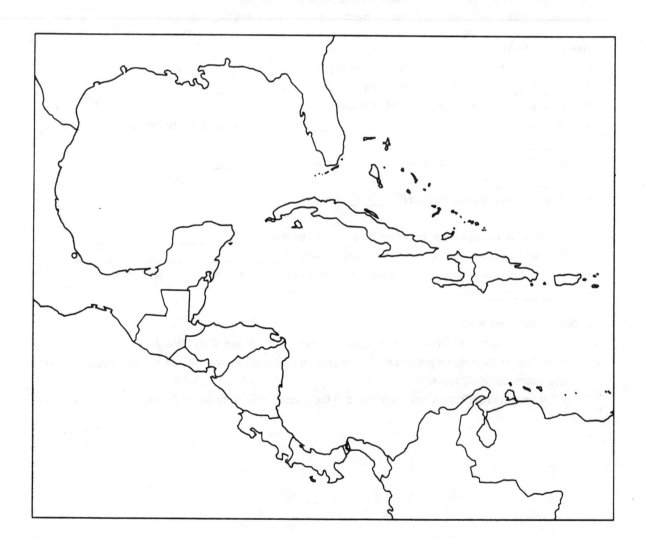

CHAPTER 22

1. Label: Grenada, Islands, Dominican Republic, Haiti, Cuba, Mexico, El Salvador, Belize, Guatemala, Virgin. Honduras, Nicaragua, Costa Rica, Panama, Canal Zone.
2. Place an X at the location of Guantanamo Bay, Jamaica, Puerto Rico, Antigua, St. Lucia, Trinidad.
3. Label: Caribbean Sea, Gulf of Mexico, Atlantic Ocean, Bay of Pigs.

READING THE MAP

1. In 1954 the CIA engineered a right-wing over-throw of the elected government in _____.

2. In 1959 revolutionaries under Fidel Castro overthrew the U.S.-backed Batista government in _____.

3. In 1961 a U.S.-backed exile army failed in its attempted invasion of Cuba at the _____.

4. In 1962 the U.S. Navy blockaded _____ to prevent the delivery of Soviet missiles to that island.

5. In 1965 President Johnson sent 20,000 Marines to support an anti-Communist junta in _____.

6. The modern Central American country of Belize was until recently a British protectorate known as _____.

7. In a 1977 treaty with the United States, Panama gained control of the _____ in 1979.

8. In 1979 the revolutionary leftist Sandinista government overthrew the U.S.-backed regime in _____.

9. In 1983, fearing a Marxist takeover of the island, President Reagan ordered a military invasion of _____.

10. In the 1980s, the Central American country of _____ served as a staging area for U.S.-backed counterrevolutionary forces fighting Nicaragua's government.

11. The 1987 Arias Central American Peace Plan was proposed by the President of _____.

12. In 1990 President Bush sent U.S. troops to _____ to arrest its president on charges of international drug dealing.

INTERPRETING THE MAP

1. How has the United States manifested its concern about the strategic location of the Caribbean nations?
2. Why has Central America become a focal point in American foreign policy in recent years?
3. For almost 100 years the United States has controlled the Panama Canal. Why did it decide to give up its lease there?

CHAPTER 23

THE END OF THE COLD WAR IN EUROPE

The Cold War shaped the foreign policy and much of the domestic politics of the United States for almost half a century. When it ended in the late 1980s, the European continent was restructured—a restructuring that had a tremendous effect on the United States and the globe. The two Germanys were reunited, Czechoslovakia split up into the Czech Republic and Slovakia, and the Soviet Union collapsed into a group of member states dominated by Russia. While the European economy remained strong, there was tremendous political uncertainty on the edges of Europe as ethnic conflict in the former Yugoslavia and uncertainty in Russia threatened to spill beyond their borders.

CHAPTER 23

1. Label the countries newly formed or reorganized as a result of the end of the Cold War:
2. Indicate with a dot and label: Sarejevo, Moscow, Berlin, Prague, and Tijana.
3. Germany, Lithuania, Latvia, Estonia, Bosnia-Herzegovina, Croatia, Slovenia, Yugoslavia, Macedonia, the Czech Republic, Slovakia.

READING THE MAP

1. The first country in which the Communists fell was _____.
2. The "velvet revolution" was in _____.
3. The country where the most U.S. soldiers and military equipment are stationed is _____.
4. The military organization of which the United States and many of its Cold War allies is called _____. This acronym stands for _____.

INTERPRETING THE MAP

1. Discuss the impact of the fall of the Soviet Union and the end of the Cold War on the politics of the United States.
2. Research declining troop levels in Europe. What countries were troops taken out of? For what strategic reasons?

CHAPTER 1: ANSWERS

THE CIVIL WAR

READING THE MAP

1. Richmond; James; York
2. Gettysburg, Pennsylvania, and Antietam, Maryland
3. Mississippi; Tennessee; Atlanta to Savannah, Georgia
4. New Orleans; Vicksburg, Mississippi
5. Henry and Donelson; Shiloh, Tennessee
6. Railroads, weapons, numbers of soldiers. Geographical size, leadership, tacit support of European allies.

INTERPRETING THE MAP

1. The location of the capital cities of the two sides, Washington, D.C., and Richmond, Virginia, are only about 100 miles apart. Both sides had to mass and maintain sizable armies to defend their respective capitals. The capture of Richmond was one of the three strategic objectives of the Union war plan.
2. Western Tennessee, where the Cumberland and Tennessee Rivers flow from south to north into the Ohio River, was an opening to the South for Union armies. Tennessee was also strategically important as a granary for the Confederacy, and Chattanooga, along with Atlanta, Georgia, was a major hub of southern railroad transportation.
3. The Confederacy had over 3,000 miles of coastline. Even with its naval superiority, the Union navy was stretched too thin to ever completely blockade all Confederate ports. Blockade running was a highly profitable enterprise for Confederate entrepreneurs.
4. At the time of the Civil War, the North was far ahead of the south in its industrialization and transportation network. With the South's few industrial sites concentrated in its important cities like Richmond and Charleston, and its railroad hub in Atlanta, the North had relatively easy targets. Likewise, by concentrating their efforts on conquering Mississippi ports like Vicksburg and New Orleans, the North could cripple Southern river transportation and cut off the Southern interiors direct access to the Atlantic and Gulf of Mexico. By contrast, even if the Confederacy had decided to pursue an offensive strategy in the war, the North's complex systems of roads, rails, canal, and rivers, as well as its multiple, geographically diversified industrial centers and ports, would have made disabling the North a most difficult proposition.

CHAPTER 2: ANSWERS

RAILROADS AND THE NEW TRANSPORTATION SYSTEMS

READING THE MAP

1. Omaha, Sacramento
2. Promontory Point, Salt Lake City, Utah

3. Southern Pacific Railroad
4. China; Ireland

INTERPRETING THE MAP

1. The opening of the transcontinental railroad helped to usher the American economy into an era of explosive growth. Both merchants and farmers found national markets for their goods; with the railroad, people and goods could move throughout the country more quickly, conveniently, and eventually more cheaply, than ever before, and farmers could get their crops and livestock to market more easily. As the railroads shaped the economy, they also shaped American society by helping to populate the West and pulling people closer together: the railroads connected the coasts with each other and with the interior of the country physically and metaphorically. The society of the West began to resemble that of the rest of the country.

2. The railroads influenced the settlement and development patterns of the United States in much the same way that explorers and their routes had in an earlier era. People settled in railroad hubs or along the railroad lines; farmers located themselves in proximity to depots from which they could shop their produce to market.

3. The transcontinental railroad ran up against the same natural hurdles that faced the wagon trains of the early nineteenth century: the Rocky Mountains, then the Sierra Nevada on the way to California and the Cascade Mountains into the Pacific Northwest, in addition to many desert areas, rivers, and hostile Indian tribes along the way. Social and political hurdles were substantial also. The railroads literally put towns on the map and very often delivered economic growth; thus, enticing a railroad to come through one's town was a goal of many western politicians. However, this increased economic activity included the businesses that serviced a transient population of railroad workers and gamblers: not only provisions and inns, but also saloons and brothels. Moral crusaders of the nineteenth century say (particularly in Utah) saw these as pernicious influences on American society and at times fought the railroads on those grounds.

4. The railroad altered the environment of the West by bringing waves of settlers and prospectors to previously unpopulated or sparsely populated lands. The railroads allowed farmers to put more land into cultivation because they made for faster access to larger markets. The railroads also, through the ever-popular bison hunt, contributed to the extermination of those animals and the Native American groups that depended on them for food.

CHAPTER 3: ANSWERS

TERRITORIAL EXPANSION TO THE CIVIL WAR

READING THE MAP

1. New Hampshire, Massachusetts, Connecticut, Rhode Island, New York, New Jersey, Pennsylvania, Delaware, Maryland, Virginia, North Carolina, South Carolina, Georgia
2. Ohio, Indiana, Illinois, Michigan, Wisconsin, (and Minnesota)
3. Kentucky, Tennessee, Alabama, Mississippi, Vermont, and Maine
4. Louisiana, Arkansas, Missouri, Iowa, North Dakota, South Dakota, Nebraska, Kansas, Oklahoma, Colorado, Wyoming, and Montana
5. Florida

6. Texas was annexed directly to statehood from it status as the independent Lone Star Republic. The territory claimed by Texas when it was annexed also include what are now portions of the states of New Mexico, Oklahoma, Kansas, Colorado, and Wyoming.
7. California, Nevada, Utah, Arizona, New Mexico, Colorado, and Wyoming
8. Washington, Oregon, Idaho, Montana, and Wyoming

INTERPRETING THE MAP

1. Pushing Native Americans further westward ahead of the American transcontinental movement affected the development of the West in many ways. For a few, it meant that certain areas would be ostensibly off-limits to settlements as they were traditional Indian lands or reservations, that life on the frontier would be dangerous and lived under the threat of Indian attack, and that the U.S. military would have a role in the settlement of the continent, as they were often needed to move Indians off lands, to establish American outposts on the frontier, and to protect settlers.
2. There are many possible answers to the question. A correctly formulated answer should be detailed and focus on one aspect of differences.

CHAPTER 4: ANSWERS

RECONSTRUCTION

READING THE MAP

1. Tennessee
2. Tennessee
3. Virginia and Georgia
4. South Carolina, Florida, and Louisiana
5. Virginia
6. North Carolina, South Carolina, Tennessee, Florida, Alabama, Arkansas, Louisiana
7. South Carolina, Florida, and Louisiana

INTERPRETING THE MAP

1. The former Confederate states were divided into military districts, each governed by an army general, as a way of maintaining law and order in the region and establishing an administrative shell under which the states could take the steps mandated by Congress for readmission.
2. Federal troops still occupied the capitals of South Carolina and Louisiana when the 1876 election was held. The so-called Compromise of 1877 allegedly included a promise by Republican candidate Rutherford B. Hayes to withdraw these troops if the Democrats assented to his election.
3. In observance of states' rights, each former Confederate state was required to draft its own state constitution and elect state officers that would satisfy congressional readmission requirements. The time it took to do this varied from state to state.

CHAPTER 5: ANSWERS

FARMERS AND THE ELECTION OF 1896

READING THE MAP
1. States won by Republican candidate William McKinley in the presidential election of 1896.
2. Midwest and Northeast
3. Five (Minnesota, Iowa, North Dakota, California, and Oregon); four (Kentucky, West Virginia, Maryland, and Delaware)
4. Bryan; Bryan; McKinley; split; split
5. 23; 22
6. St. Louis, Missouri

INTERPRETING THE MAP
1. Much of McKinley's success in the Midwest may be attributed to the factor that compared to the South and the Plains states, the Midwest (like the Northeast) had more urban voters, who as a group tended to vote Republican in 1896. One reason for this was that urban workers had little to gain from Bryan's free-silver stance: it would have inflated food prices for urban consumers. Another reason was that urban ethnics were repulsed by the anti-immigrant position earlier taken by the Populist party and by Bryan's evangelical style. A final reason was that Midwest farmers, with their greater diversity of crops, were better off than both the wheat farmers of the Plains and southern cotton farmers. Thus, they were less attracted to the agrarian "radicalism" offered by Bryan.
2. Bryan was enthusiastically supported by the silver-mining interests in the western states. Since Bryan promised to adopt the bimetallic standard of gold and silver, silver-mining interests stood to gain an assured market for their metal at the government mint.
3. The presidency is decided by the winning of electoral-college votes. Bryan and McKinley won a near equal number of states in 1896, but those won by McKinley were concentrated in the much more populous Northeast and Midwest. The distribution of electoral college votes is based on congressional representation, which is based on state population, so McKinley defeated Bryan handily in the electoral college, 271 to 176.
4. One of the major reasons for women gaining the right to vote in certain western states so long before they did in the East was the nature of frontier life. The gender roles observed elsewhere were not compatible with the western environment, where by necessity men and women, husbands and wives, had to work as partners to make a living from the land and survive with the constant threat of attack from Indians and Spanish settlers in the Southwest. The more equal division of duties often translated to an increase in rights accorded women in the West.

CHAPTER 6: ANSWERS

AMERICAN EMPIRE

READING THE MAP

1. Philippine Islands; Puerto Rico
2. Alaska and the Midway Islands
3. South America
4. Alaska
5. The Philippines and Guam; Puerto Rico

INTERPRETING THE MAP

1. Attaching Spain in the Philippines rather than Cuba puzzle was a matter of preparation. Admiral Dewey's fleet was in Hong Kong, 600 miles from the Philippines when the war began. He was under orders to capture the Philippines if war was declared. (Actually, Dewey's fleet gained control only of Manila. As the commander of a naval force he was not prepared to occupy the whole Philippines archipelago.) American forces were not so readily prepared to conquer Cuba, even though it was a target nearer to the United States. Logistical snafus also slowed the invasion force preparing to invade Cuba.

2. The Philippines is an archipelago—a collection of scattered islands not easily occupied by invading forces. The wide dispersal of the population over these islands complicated U.S. efforts at pacification. Also, the jungle terrain and heavy rains in these islands magnified the difficulty of successfully suppressing the skilled guerrilla fighters of the insurrection. But the length of the conflict was not only a result of geography and climate: the Filipinos fought with higher morale and greater tenacity to achieve their independence from the United States than the Spaniards did to save their empire in 1898.

3. Seward knew that Alaska's purchase would bring the United States a bounty of natural resources, possibly encourage British Columbia (lying between Alaska and Washington Territory) to join the United States, and, perhaps most importantly, keep the British from buying Alaska. Seward's plan was for the United States to gain possession of all North American ports to assure American dominance of the Pacific and Far East trade.

CHAPTER 7: ANSWERS

THE UNITED STATES IN ASIA, 1900–1940

READING THE MAP

1. Alaska
2. Philippine Islands
3. Hawaii, Wake, and Guam
4. China
5. Korea
6. Russia, China proper, Korea

INTERPRETING THE MAP

1. With its victory in the Spanish-American War, the United States became a possessor of Asian territory—the Philippines. Some Americans saw opportunities to use this new Asian possession as a stepping-stone to the "China market," where they hoped to sell American surplus goods. As a

consequence, the United States adopted an "Open Door" (free-trade) policy to guide its relations with Asian nations for the next half century. In addition, Americans saw in Asia an opportunity to extend their empire further, in essence, a chance to make Americans of the "uncivilized" Asians. Just as they had pursued Manifest Destiny across the North American continent, Americans saw themselves just as inevitable carrying on right across the Pacific.

2. In deference to Japan's power in the area, the United States conceded to it territorial dominance in some parts of Asia. In the Taft-Katsura Agreement of 1905, the United States recognized Japan's hegemony in Korea in return for a Japanese promise to invade the Philippines or challenge America's rights there. In the 1908 Root-Takahira Agreement, the United States recognized Japanese interests in Manchuria while both countries supported Chinese independence otherwise and upheld Open Door, essentially confirming the status quo in the region. At the Washington Naval Conference in 1921–1922, these agreements were reaffirmed.

3. The Japanese considered their control of Manchuria a vital buffer against Russia, and a source of food and key raw materials like coal and timber. Japan had a population of over 65 million inhabiting an area about the size of Texas; it was constantly in search of guaranteed access to raw materials. After the Japanese invasion of Manchuria in 1931, the United States refused to recognize the Japanese puppet government there through the Stimson Doctrine. When Japan invaded China proper in 1937, President Roosevelt called for the quarantining of aggressor nations (Japan) and sent loans and military equipment to China. But with a dangerous war shaping up in Europe, American leaders were unwilling to take stronger measures that might precipitate war with Japan.

CHAPTER 8: ANSWERS

THE UNITED STATES IN LATIN AMERICA, 1900–1930

READING THE MAP

1. Puerto Rico (1898); Puerto Rico, Canal Zone (1903), and Guantanamo naval base (1903); Puerto Rico, Canal Zone, Guantanamo naval base, and the Virgin Islands (1916)
2. United States, Mexico, Cuba
3. a. Mexico, Belize (formerly British Honduras), Guatemala, Honduras, Nicaragua, Costa Rica
   b. Panama, Colombia, Venezuela
   c. Cuba, Haiti, Dominican Republic, Puerto Rico, Virgin Islands
4. Cuba
5. Atlantic Ocean (through the Caribbean Sea) and Pacific Ocean

INTERPRETING THE MAP

1. President McKinley, Congress, and the American public were enthusiastic about the prospect of annexing Cuba when the Spanish-American War ended. However, the humanitarian-inspired Teller Amendment (1898) pledged that the United States would not annex Cuba. In addition, the outbreak of insurrection in the Philippines cooled some of the annexation enthusiasm; many anti-imperialists warned that the annexation of Cuba would produce insurrection there as well.
2. For many congressmen, Nicaragua seemed to be the best choice for a canal. Though wider than Panama, it contained several navigable inland lakes and rivers and the actual miles of construction— fifty— would be about the same as a canal through Panama. But Congress selected Panama, in part

because it was frightened by the prospect of volcanic activity and earthquakes in Nicaragua. Also, American engineers made a case for the easier and less-costly construction and maintenance of a canal through Panama. Ships sailing through the Panama route would have a passage time about one-third shorter than they would by a Nicaraguan canal.

3. The Platt Amendment (1901), which made Cuba a virtual protectorate of the United States, became an appendix to the Cuban constitution. It guaranteed that the United States could buy or lease Cuban territory for coaling stations or naval bases. In 1903 an American naval base was leased at Guantanamo Bay on the southeastern coast of Cuba, and it is still there today.

4. This is a complex question and there are many possible answers. Correct answers should pay attention to the strategic importance of the Panama Canal for shipping and raw materials, including wood and fruit produced in the region.

5. American investment, transportation networks, and strategic interests played an important role in motivating the United States to intervene in Central America and the Caribbean.

CHAPTER 9: ANSWERS

IMMIGRATION

READING THE MAP

1. England, Scotland, Ireland, Germany, Norway, and Sweden
2. Italy, Greece, and Russia
3. Northern and western Europe; southern and eastern Europe
4. Southern and eastern Europe
5. 1882; 1915
6. big cities
7. Japan or China

INTERPRETING THE MAP

1. The explosion of European immigration to the United States in the late nineteenth and early twentieth centuries was greatly facilitate by transportation advances. Railroads made the would-be immigrant's journey to a port city much faster, easier, and cheaper; American railroads could likewise, take him from his port of entry to where he was to settle. And even more important than the railroad was the advent of the steamship, which greatly reduced the time and cost of transatlantic travel. Among the environmental causes of immigration to America were improvements in medicine and pubic health as well as natural disasters in Europe in the late nineteenth and early twentieth centuries. Europe experienced a precipitous mid- to late-century decline in infant mortality, which resulted in later food and land shortages. Facing such pressures, many poorer Europeans saw a brighter future in America. Exacerbating these problems were the catastrophes that befell southern Italy in the first decade of the twentieth century: a string of earthquakes, volcanic eruptions, and even a tidal wave devastated the region in rapid succession.

2. "New" immigrants to America tended to settle in large cities in the Northeast, Middle Atlantic states, and Upper North Central states—the core "urban zone." In these industrial areas, unskilled and semi-skilled "new" immigrants found jobs. By 1920 three-fourths of all foreign born in America lived in

cities, and one-half of all city dwellers were either foreign born or children of foreign-born parents. Furthermore, big cities (at least on the East Coast) were immigrants' ports of entry, and many immigrants, being too poor to move on, simply settled there. Thus as a result of the industrial jobs to be had in the cities ad settlement by default, many American cities developed large, close-knit ethnic communities that offered later immigrants some comfort in vestiges of the old country as they adjusted to America.

3. America's major source of immigrants shifted from northern and western Europe to southern and eastern Europe. This shift occurred in part because industrial development in Germany and Sweden slowed immigration, while Canada and Australia attracted many immigrants from the British Isles. On the other hand, increased religious and political persecution in southern and eastern Europe combined with the removal of ancient emigration restraints there to open the doors to migration. America's offer of economic opportunity and the relatively inexpensive passage available on railroads and steamships made migration there a reasonable choice.

CHAPTER 10: ANSWERS

THE UNITED STATES IN WORLD WAR I

READING THE MAP

1. Germany, Austria-Hungary, Bulgaria, and Ottoman Empire (Turkey).
2. Britain, France, and Russia formed the original Triple Entente before the war. Later joining the Allies, as they came to be know, were Albania, Romania, Belgium, Portugal, Greece, and several Baltic and North African states.
3. Until Russia left the war in 1918, Germany had to fight the Russians on the eastern front and the British, French, and Americans on the western front.
4. France
5. North Sea
6. In the Atlantic Ocean off the coast of France and around the British Isles, including the English Channel.

INTERPRETING THE MAP

1. Most Americans felt at ease that the Atlantic Ocean safely separated them from the calamity that befell Europe in 1914. Most people had sentimental favorites whom they hoped might win the war, but overwhelmingly, Americans rejoiced in their physical isolation from Europe and in President Wilson's proclamation of neutrality.
2. The west front ran a 400-mile course through northern France from the English Channel to Switzerland. For the most part it was a relatively flat landscape, but on its eastern end it also contained hilly wooded areas through which ran many streams and rivers. Both sides built elaborate trenches along the front, where they dug in and slugged it out during four years of war.
3. The Zimmermann telegram appeared to pose a territorial threat to the United States. The note informed Mexico that in the event of war between Germany and the United States, Germany would be pleased to see Mexico take back Texas and the territorial cession Mexico made to the United States at the end of the Mexican War in 1848. For many Americans, this revelation drove home the potential

danger of a German victory, and it encouraged President Wilson to abandon neutrality and ask Congress for a declaration of war.

CHAPTER 11: ANSWERS

AFRICAN-AMERICAN MIGRATION

READING THE MAP

1. Washington, D.C.
2. Florida
3. railroad
4. Chicago, East St. Louis, Washington, D.C.

INTERPRETING THE MAP

1. The causes of the Great Migration include the unrelenting repression, exemplified by the sharecropping system and Jim Crow laws, that blacks lived under in the South as well as low cotton process and a boll weevil epidemic. Migration, already steady since the end of the Civil War, spiked during World War I. With many white men in the service and immigration interrupted by the war, job opportunities opened up for blacks in the factories and stockyards of the North.
2. The Great Migration had a significant effect on the American economy. The South lost much of it labor pool and, with immigration regulation relaxed, began to turn to Mexicans for cheap agricultural labor. More important and visible, though, was the effect it had in the North. Just as the South's was weakened, the North's labor pool drew strength from the influx of workers from the South. But the Great Migration also had its negative side: many old Americans saw the new arrivals threatening the culture and fabric of the cities while immigrants saw them as competition for jobs. This, in turn, provoked racist and discriminatory reactions against blacks. While never to be institutionalized as in the South, racism in the North was no less insidious.

CHAPTER 12: ANSWERS

EUROPE BETWEEN THE WARS

READING THE MAP

1. Finland, Estonia, Latvia, Lithuania, Poland, Czechoslovakia, Yugoslavia, Austria, and Hungary
2. France, Italy, Greece, Rumania, Belgium, Denmark
3. Germany, Bulgaria, Soviet Union
4. Yugoslavia, Czechoslovakia
5. Montenegro, Serbia
6. Soviet Union
7. Denmark, Belgium, France, Poland, Czechoslovakia, Lithuania
8. Poland

1. The so-called Polish Corridor between Germany and East Prussia was intended to give Poland access to the Baltic Sea port at Danzig (modern Gdansk), which was established as a Free City.
2. The north-to-south string of new nations in eastern Europe (from Finland south through Poland to Yugoslavia) was intended to serve both as a guardian for the USSR against German aggression from the west, and as a liberal-nationalist barrier against Bolshevik expansion from the Soviet Union in the east.
3. Because President Wilson insisted on the principle of national self-determination, attention was paid to the historic nationalities of the people of Europe. It proved impossible to apply this criterion precisely, as national groups were scattered all over the Continent. And contrary to the rule, Germany was forced to give up significant amounts of territory that was inhabited largely by Germans (Rhineland, Alsace- Lorraine, Saar Basin, Sudetenland, Danzig, Polish Corridor).

CHAPTER 13: ANSWERS

NEW CONSUMERISM AND GENDER ROLES IN THE 1920S: A SEARS HOUSE

READING THE MAP
1. indirect
2. public transporation—the streetcar or subway.

INTERPRETING THE MAP
1. New technology in the Sears house included running water in the bathroom and the kitchen, electric gas range, a refrigerator, a gramaphone and electronic lighting.
2. This house design is spacious and designed for a small family living in the suburbs.
3. This house includes plenty of living space, privacy, and new eletrical appliances for entertainment, food preparation and hygiene.
4. Note that much of the new technology in the Sears house affects the woman's or private sphere of the house. Note too that that woman's portion of the house--the kitchen--is separated by ten feet from the public part of the house--the living room and the porch.
5. It was designed for 1 or 2 children not the larger families that were popular in the nineteenth century.

CHAPTER 14: ANSWERS

WORLD WAR II IN EUROPE AND NORTH AFRICA

READING THE MAP
1. Germany and Italy
2. Great Britain and the Soviet Union (USSR)
3. Portugal, Spain, Switzerland, Sweden

4. English Channel; Normandy coast in northern France
5. Egypt
6. Casablanca, Cairo, Teheran, Yalta
7. Stalingrad

INTERPRETING THE MAP

1. The North Africa campaign was intended to keep the German armies from capturing the Suez Canal and advancing into the Middle East. By gaining control of North Africa, the Allies were in a position to invade Sicily and then Italy. The collapse of Italy opened the Mediterranean Sea to Allied shipping, gave the Allies access to air bases close enough to bomb German-held territory in the Balkans and central Europe, and allowed the Allies to take the offensive on the Continent.
2. Stalingrad was strategically important as a major industrial city. It also protected the southern flank of the Soviet capital of Moscow as well as access to the Middle East via the Volga River and Caspian Sea. The battle of Stalingrad also marked the high-water mark of Hitler's eastern-theater campaign. When Stalingrad held, the Russians began an offensive that culminated in the Red Army's occupation of Berlin in 1945.
3. The landing area for the cross-Channel invasion of Europe in 1944 had to meet several requirements. It had to be close enough to England to be within range of fighter planes that could supply air support, it had to have at least one major port, and the landing beaches had to be sheltered from winds. The Normandy coast between Caen and Cherbourg in northern France was selected.

CHAPTER 15: ANSWERS

WORLD WAR II IN THE PACIFIC

READING THE MAP

1. Burma, Thailand, French Indochina (Vietnam, Laos, and Cambodia), Korea,
2. Netherlands (Dutch) East Indies; Philippines; New Guinea; and the Solomons
3. Hawaiian Islands (at Pearl Harbor)
4. Aleutian (Alaska); Marshall and Gilbert; Solomon Islands
5. Iwo Jima and Okinawa
6. Australia and New Zealand
7. Philippines

INTERPRETING THE MAP

1. Distances were great in the Pacific campaign. From Hawaii, where the first attack occurred, to Japan, scene of the last, is a distance of over 4,000 miles. In order to win the war, it was thus of critical strategic importance, that the United States gain possession of islands close enough to launch air attacks on Japan's home islands. This was first accomplished in July, 1944 with the capture of Saipan in the Marianas (1,350 miles from Tokyo, a 17-hour round trip by bomber), and later when the U.S. took Iwo Jima (750 miles) and Okinawa (350 miles).
2. By recapturing the Philippines, the United States severed Japan's supply, and communications lines with the raw materials–rich Indochina, Malaya, and Dutch East Indies. The Philippines were also to be used as the staging area for the planned invasion of the Japanese home islands in 1945.

3. Iwo Jima is shaped like a pork chop. Its narrow end is dominated by 546-foot Mt. Suribachi, while the rest of the island is a broad plateau easily covered by artillery and mortar fire from the mountain. The only suitable landing beaches were near Mt. Suribachi, and thus were vulnerable to Japanese gun emplacements. The U.S. Marines had to take the mountain in order to gain control of the airfield in the middle of the island. Once captured, that airfield launched fighter-plane escorts and B-29s for fire-bomb raids over Japan.

4. As they pursued Japan across the Pacific toward the home island, the Allies made significant strategic gains that strengthened their efforts. Recapturing the Philippines and Southeast Asia not only cut Japan's communications to its outposts in the area and its supply lines, it also gave the Allies control of the very raw materials that had made the region so valuable to Japan. This, along with the capture of strategically located Pacific islands, also put the Allies in position to attack the Japanese home islands, overcoming the daunting geographical distances that had hindered the early conduct of the campaign. Moreover, the nature of the war in the Pacific forced technological innovation in naval and aerial warfare, the manufacture and design of ships and planes, and weaponry—the best example of which is the development and use of the atomic bomb.

CHAPTER 16: ANSWERS

THE COLD WAR IN EUROPE

READING THE MAP

1. Poland, Czechoslovakia, Hungary, Rumania, Bulgaria, Yugoslavia, Albania, Germany (divided among Allies)
2. Poland
3. Greece and Turkey
4. France and Italy
5. Berlin
6. Hungary
7. Germany

INTERPRETING THE MAP

1. In a crucial territorial decision, the Big Three agreed to the division of Germany into three occupation zones that in 1948 became East and West Germany. In addition, Poland's borders were shifted to the west. The Soviet Union, for security reasons, demanded eastern Poland to the so-called Curzon Line. As compensation for their loss, the Poles were given chunks of eastern Germany to the Neisse and Oder Rivers. Austria and Czechoslovakia were restored to full independence from Germany.

2. Following the battle of Stalingrad in 1942, the Soviet Union gained the offensive against Germany's army and the Red Army moved on a broad front into eastern Europe. When the war ended in 1945, Soviet troops occupied Eastern Europe. Stalin, noting that Germany had twice invaded Russia in the twentieth century, insisted that the countries separating the USSR from Germany have governments that were "friendly" to the Soviet Union and that they act as a Soviet sphere of influence to shield Soviet borders from any future European attack.

3. Greece and Turkey are strategically as they control the Bosporus and Dardanelles straits leading from the Black Sea into the Aegean Sea. Western bloc control of these straits would enable it to contain

3. North Vietnam; Laos
4. Demilitarized Zone (DMZ); 17th (17° N latitude)
5. Gulf of Tonkin; North Vietnam
6. Laos and Cambodia

INTERPRETING THE MAP

1. While it was not usually presented to the American public as a rationale for U.S. involvement in Vietnam, some presidential advisers in the 1960s believed Vietnam was intrinsically important to U.S. security interests in Asia. This argument was based on Vietnam's location in relation to India, China, and Japan, and on its proximity to the sea routes of the South China Sea—the major arena for trade and naval operations in Southeast Asia. These advisers saw Vietnam as an outpost for a forward defense of U.S. interests in the Pacific, and feared that if Communist Chinese influence dominated the Southeast Asian peninsula on which Vietnam is located, American security interests would be threatened. The idea was that if Vietnam fell to communism, the rest of Southeast Asia would follow. This was known as the "domino theory."
2. South Vietnam was 9,000 miles from the United States. It had long land and coastal borders that proved impossible to seal against infiltration and attack. Further, weather and terrain conditions in South Vietnam also presented major obstacles to military operations and logistical support. Vietnam lies entirely within the tropics, where intense heat and irregular but heavy rains often inhibited military maneuvers. In addition, most of South Vietnam was covered with dense jungle and rugged mountains that further complicated troop and equipment movement on the ground. That is why guerrilla tactics and the helicopter played such key roles in the Vietnam War.
3. The 1954 Geneva Convention divided former French Indochina into North and South Vietnam along the 17th parallel. This was originally intended as a temporary measure; national unification elections were supposed to be held in 1956. But, fearing a victory by the Vietnamese nationalist hero and Communist Ho Chi Minh, the United States and South Vietnamese governments refused to cooperate with the scheduled elections. Eventually, then, Vietnam came to be unified by the bullet, not by the ballot.

CHAPTER 20 ANSWERS

IMMIGRATION 1950–1990

READING THE MAP

1. Northwestern Europe; Latin America; Latin America; Latin America
2. Asia; Asia; northwestern Europe; northwestern Europe
3. Latin America; Asia; roughly equal between Latin America and Asia
4. Latin America; southeastern Europe
5. Latin America and Asia
6. Northwestern Europe

INTERPRETING THE MAP

1. The United States maintained its tight immigration-restriction quotas during and just after World War II. This sharply limited the number of European immigrants, especially from war-ravaged

southern and eastern Europe. Even in the liberalizing Displaced Persons Act of 1948, the United States discriminated against Jews. However, the creation of Israel in 1948 attracted many European Jews who might otherwise have come to the United States. Immigration laws were suspended in 1956 to allow thousands of refugees from the failed Hungarian Revolt to enter the United States. Finally, in 1965 the immigration quotas were removed from the law, opening wider doors for immigrants from southeastern Europe and Asia.

2. Thousands of Mexican immigrants came to the United States as participants in the *bracero* program to supply farm laborers to the fields during World War II. Mexicans trying to escape poverty have continued to seek entrance since then, and many have come as illegal aliens without proper documentation. Puerto Ricans came to fill the low-wage job openings on the East Coast, especially in New York City in the 1950s and 1960s. They were unique among immigrants in that they already were American citizens when they arrived. Refugees from Castro's Cuban Revolution flooded into Miami after 1959, and refugees from the Central American wars in El Salvador and Nicaragua have arrived more recently.

3. While many of American's Asian immigrants were refugees from war and revolution, most came seeking economic opportunity. The largest flood of Asian immigrants recently has been the refugees from Vietnam following the collapse of South Vietnam's government in 1975.

CHAPTER 21: ANSWER

TH UNITED STATES AND THE MIDDLE EAST

READING THE MAP

1. Red Sea and Mediterranean Sea
2. None
3. Iran
4. Commonwealth of Independent States (former USSR); Persian Gulf
5. Iraq, Iran, Saudi Arabia
6. Egypt, Jordan, Syria, and Lebanon
7. Jordan River
8. Persian Gulf and Gulf of Oman
9. Iraq

INTERPRETING THE MAP

1. The modern nation of Israel was created in 1948 from British-held Palestine. The possessed Palestinians, together with Arab Middle Eastern nations, have posed a constant threat to Israeli's existence, and there has been frequent conflict between the Palestinians and their powerful Arab allies and Israel. To enhance its security in these hostile surroundings, Israel has consistently refused to restore territory it captured in the Six Day War in 1967, including the West Bank from Jordan, the Golan Heights from Syria, and the Gaza Strip and Sinai Peninsula from Egypt. (The Sinai was returned to Egypt in the Camp David accords in 1978.)

2. The nations of the Middle East link three continents. They stand astride the vital land, air, and water routes to Europe, Asia, and Africa. The area also controls three vital water links; the Suez Canal, the Bosporus and Dardanelles straits, and the Strait of Hormuz. For the United States and its postwar containment policy, the Middle East, Iran in particular, served as a buffer between the Soviet Union and warm-water ports that would have given the Soviets access to the Indian Ocean and Mediterranean Sea.

3. Operation Desert Storm's ground war operation that liberated Kuwait from occupation by Iraqi forces in less than 100 hours was preceded by several weeks of air war. Both operations benefited from the barren desert environment in the region. The desert terrain allowed U.N. coalition air forces to easily locate enemy targets. Iraq had no natural cover to hide its vital road and rail links to troops in Kuwait, nor could they conceal the vehicles that traveled on them. Rapid deployment and maneuver (such as the envelopment maneuver fashioned by coalition commanders to avoid the Iraqi army's strongest defenses) was also facilitated by the desert terrain.

CHAPTER 22: ANSWERS

THE UNITED STATES, CENTRAL AMERICA AND THE CARIBBEAN

READING THE MAP

1. Guatemala	7. Canal Zone
2. Cuba	8. Nicaragua
3. Bay of Pigs	9. Grenada
4. Cuba	10. Honduras
5. Dominican Republic	11. Costa Rica
6. British Honduras	12. Panama

INTERPRETING THE MAP

1. In the twentieth century the United States has tried to deny potential enemies access to passageways through the islands along the eastern rim of the Caribbean. From Florida to Venezuela, these islands form a kind of "picket fence" defense for the Gulf of Mexico and the Caribbean Sea, and they form the edge of a defensive buffer for the Canal Zone. These considerations led the United States to acquire Puerto Rico; maintain a naval base at Guantanamo Bay; purchase the Virgin Islands from Denmark in 1917; lease bases in Jamaica, St. Lucia, Antigua, and Trinidad (not all are active today); support an invasion of the Bay of Pigs in Cuba in 1961; intervene in the Dominican Republic in 1965; and invade Grenada in 1983 and Panama in 1990.

2. In the 1980s, the Reagan administration formed a premise that the political unrest in Central America was caused by Soviet influence. More concrete evidence of Cuban aid to leftist insurgents in El Salvador and Nicaragua brought American intervention. The United States supported Honduran-based pro-American counterrevolutionary (Contra) military forces in an attempt to overthrow the leftist Sandinista government in Nicaragua. By the end of the decade, domestic opposition to this policy, the military failures of the Contras, a cooling of Cold War rhetoric, and a Central American Peace Plan initiated by Costa Rica's President Arias forced abandonment of the United States' proxy war in Nicaragua. The United States also was covertly involved in wars in El Salvador and Guatemala.

3. In 1977, President Carter saw the restoration of Panamanian sovereignty over the Canal Zone as an apology for past wrongdoing (given the manner in which the United States acquired its lease),and as an expression of goodwill hoping to create an atmosphere of trust that would render other Latin American problems more easily solved. Conclusion of a treaty gave Panama sovereignty over the Canal Zone in 1979 and the promise of its control over the canal itself in 1999 (though the United States retains the right to protect the canal). It did not, as Carter had hoped, have a meliorating impact on unrest in Central America.

CHAPTER 23: ANSWERS

THE END OF THE COLD WAR IN EUROPE

READING THE MAP
1. Poland
2. Czechoslovakia
3. Germany
4. NATO. North Atlantic Treaty Organization

INTERPRETING THE MAP
1. Without the Soviet Union and related Cold War themes to rely on, American politics lost rhetorical staples that had served it well for fifty years. American politics lost rhetorical staples that had served it well for fifty years. In light of this, American foreign policy had to be rethought; the disappearances of the old enemy forced the reevaluation of alliances, motives, and strategies. Military spending and planning likewise had to be cast in new unfamiliar terms. Domestically, one of the fallouts of the end of the Cold War was the so-called peace dividend, the money saved by reduced Pentagon expenditures and thus theoretically available for other needs. Minus the military threat posed by the Soviet Union, Americans' attention turned to economic matters domestic and global, taking stock of America's place in the world economy and their own situations. American politicians of the post-Cold War era therefore had to address these concerns by making sense of what George Bush called the "new world order," which they did with varying degrees of success.

Page References

Chapter 1: The Civil War

	Martin, et. al. *America and Its Peoples*, 3/e	Nash/Jeffrey, *The American People*, 4/e	Divine, et. al. *America Past and Present*, 4/e	Wilson, et. al. *Pursuit of Liberty*, 3/e	Garraty, *The American Nation*, 9/e
Mapping America					
Question 1.	498, 513	513, 514, 524	453, 455, 462, 463, 465	532, 533, 534, 535, 543, 546, 547, 548	394, 396, 403, 410
Question 2.	front endpaper	513, 514, 524	rear endpaper, 446, 453, 455	532, 533, 534, 547	356, 394, 396, 410
Question 3.	513	524	465	547	—
Question 4.	280–83, 380	325, 451	350, 360, 363–63	499	231, 317, 356
Reading the Map					
Question 1.	499	512–13	453, 455	534	395, 396
Question 2.	498, 513	513, 524	455, 462	534, 535, 542–44	396, 397, 403
Question 3.	496, 516–18	513–14, 524–25	463–64, 465	531, 546, 547	394–95, 408–9
Question 4.	498, 500–501	515, 524	453, 461–62	533	394, 403–5
Question 5.	498, 500	514	452, 453	—	394, 395
Question 6.	491–95	507	444–47	530–31	388–89
Interpreting the Map					
Question 1.	498	508, 511	446	532, 534	396
Question 2.	498, 500–501	513–14	452–53	533	—
Question 3.	497	515	446	531	383, 388–89
Question 4.	280–83, 377–79, 380, 382–83, 393–95, 397–98, 493, 516–18	507	447	530	356, 388–89

Chapter 2: Railroads and New Transportation Systems

	Martin, et. al.	Nash/Jeffrey	Divine, et. al.	Wilson, et. al.	Garraty
Mapping America					
Question 1.	—	—	—	—	231
Question 2.	—	619	540	151	475
Question 3.	front endpaper	325, 619	rear endpaper,	151	356, 475
Question 4.	380	451	523, 531	151	475
Reading the Map					
Question 1.	—	619	541	146, 151	471–72, 475
Question 2.	—	619	542	147, 151	473, 475
Question 3.	—	619	543	151	471–72, 475
Question 4.	—	626	542	146, 147	472
Interpreting the Map					
Question 1.	568–69	323, 578–89	526–31	146–51	464–75
Question 2.	568–69, 586–87	323, 578–89	538–45	146–51	470–73, 476
Question 3.	front endpaper, 504, 558, 568–69, 572, 581	—	540–45	151	470–73
Question 4.	568–69, 572, 581, 586–87	578–89	532, 537–543	146–59	470–73

Chapter 3: Territorial Expansion to the Civil War

	Martin, et. al.	Nash/Jeffrey	Divine, et. al.	Wilson, et. al.	Garraty
Mapping America					
Question 1.	190, 420	438	xxviii, xxix, xxx 344	257, 285, 354, 489, 499	126, 198, 331
Question 2.	554	592	509	II.134	462
Reading the Map					
Question 1.	190	438	xxxii	245, 257	126
Question 2.	190, 420	438	xxxiii, 344	257, 500	126, 198, 331
Question 3.	190, 420	438	xxxiii, 344	257, 500	126, 331
Question 4.	420	438	344	285, 529	167, 475
Question 5.	420	278	344	354	197, 198
Question 6.	420, 430–31	438, 440	346–48	490	331
Question 7.	420	438, 442–43	344	499	331
Question 8.	420	438, 443–44	344	499	331
Interpreting the Map					
Question 1.	229–30, 307, 312–15, 417–19, 552–57, 582–83	289–95, 404–5, 461–64, 589–95596	506–13	151–56	460–62, 464

| Question 2. | 419–27, 430–35, 580–81, 584–87, 662–68 | 280–89, 351–56, 452–61, 578–89, 605–11 | 526–32 | 157–59 | 459, 468–77, 513–14 |

Chapter 4: Reconstruction

	Martin, et. al.	Nash/Jeffrey	Divine, et. al.	Wilson, et. al.	Garraty
Mapping America					
Question 1.	547	—	497	—	426
Question 2.	547	563	497	592	426
Reading the Map					
Question 1.	547	563, 570	497	592	424, 426
Question 2.	547	563, 570	497	592	424
Question 3.	547	563	497	592	426
Question 4.	547	563, 570	497	592	426
Question 5.	547	563	497	592	426
Question 6.	547	563	497	592	426
Question 7.	547	563, 570	497	592	426
Interpreting the Map					
Question 1.	—	550	—	583	424
Question 2.	—	—	496	—	439
Question 3.	538	550	479	583, 586–87 (v II pp 31, 43–35)	424

Chapter 5: Farmers and the Election of 1896

	Martin, et. al.	Nash/Jeffrey	Divine, et. al.	Wilson, et. al. (vol. II)	Garraty
Mapping America					
Question 1.	380	—	531	151	338
Question 2.	655, 730	683	601, 696	—	576
Question 3.	front endpaper	683	xxxiv	—	356
Question 4.	front endpaper	—	rear endpaper	—	356, 475
Reading the Map					
Question 1.	—	683	624	73	576
Question 2.	—	683	624	73, 75	576, 577
Question 3.	—	683	624	73	576
Question 4.	—	—	531, 624	—	338, 576
Question 5.	—	683	624	73	576
Question 6.	—	623, 683	624, A–43	—	—
Interpreting the Map					
Question 1.	—	684	—		577
Question 2.	—	—	—	75	575
Question 3.	—	683, 684	624	73	577
Question 4.	—	672	—	—	592

Chapter 6: American Empire

	Martin, et. al.	Nash/Jeffrey	Divine, et. al.	Wilson, et. al.	Garraty
Mapping America					
Question 1.	691, 708, 748, rear endpaper	699, 714	rear endpaper, 735	275	613, 619
Question 2.	705, rear endpaper	703, 714	646, 647, 735	270	613
Question 3.	705, 748, rear endpaper	703, 714	646, 647	270, 275	613, 619
Reading the Map					
Question 1.	708	699	652	275	—
Question 2.	685, 708	699	637, 652	275	607
Question 3.	694	693	635	266–67	608–9
Question 4.	708	699	652	275	623
Question 5.	704, 708	702	647	271	614, 616
Interpreting the Map					
Question 1.	—	700–701	645	267–71	612
Question 2.	708, 709–11	702	647	241–61, 267–71	616–17
Question 3.	708	691	634, rear endpaper	275	—

Chapter 7: The United States in Asia, 1900–1940

	Martin, et. al.	Nash/Jeffrey	Divine, et. al.	Wilson, et. al.	Garraty
Mapping America					
Question 1.	—	699, 716	rear endpaper	385	—
Reading the Map					
Question 1.	708	699, 716	652	275	—
Question 2.	708	699, 716	646, 652	275, 385	615
Question 3.	708	699, 716	652	275	758

Question 4.	708, rear endpaper	699, 716	652, rear endpaper	385	758
Question 5.	rear endpaper	716	rear endpaper	385	758
Question 6.	—	716	—	385	758
Interpreting the Map					
Question 1.	685–88, 689–90, 705–6, 744–45	711	631–32, 651–52	262–66	615, 620
Question 2.	860	715–17	732, 820–21	—	620–21, 697–98
Question 3.	825, 860, 863	881	820–21, 827–28	396	700–701, 743

Chapter 8: The United States in Latin America, 1900–1930

	Martin, et. al.	Nash/Jeffrey	Divine, et. al.	Wilson, et. al.	Garraty
Mapping America					
Question 1.	748	714	735	275	613, 619
Question 2.	748	714	735	275	613, 619
Question 3.	748	714	735	275	619
Reading the Map					
Question 1.	748	714	735	275	619
Question 2.	748	714	735	275	619
Question 3.	748	714	735	275	619
Question 4.	748	714	735	275	619
Question 5.	748	714	731, 735	275	619, 623
Interpreting the Map					
Question 1.	698, 705	701	642	271	614
Question 2.	745	709	730	272	621–23
Question 3.	—	710	651	—	618
Question 4.	744–48	696–97, 706–10	731, 733–34	262–66, 272–73	607–16, 617–20, 621–23, 700
Question 5.	—	—	—	—	—

Chapter 9: Immigration, 1870–1930

	Martin, et. al.	Nash/Jeffrey	Divine, et. al.	Wilson, et. al.	Garraty
Mapping America					
Question 1.	608	—	—	—	—
Question 2.	front endpaper	—	—	—	356
Question 3.	front endpaper	—	—	—	—
Question 4.	608	—	—	—	—
Reading the Map					
Question 1.	608	624	573	107–8	519
Question 2.	608	624	573	107–8	519
Question 3.	608, A–29	626	573	108	518
Question 4.	608, A–29	626	573	108	518
Question 5.	—	626	571, 673	—	518
Question 6.	616	624–27	571–72	107	517–18
Question 7.	610, 614	626	573	109	—
Interpreting the Map					
Question 1.	607–11	624–25	571–72, 672	108	517, 519
Question 2.	607–11,	625	571–72, 672	107, 109	517–19
Question 3.	607–11	624–25	571–72	107–8	517–19

Chapter 10: The United States in World War I

	Martin, et. al.	Nash/Jeffrey	Divine, et. al.	Wilson et. al.	Garraty
Mapping America					
Question 1.	760	767, 787	736	278, 282	652
Question 2.	760	767	736	278	652
Question 3.	778	787	746	282	652
Question 4.	760, 778	787	736, 746	282	652
Reading the Map					
Question 1.	760	766, 767	735, 736	277, 278	639
Question 2.	760	766, 767	735, 736	277, 278	639
Question 3.	760–61	767	736	277, 278	644
Question 4.	778	784, 787	746	282	652–53
Question 5.	760	767	736	278	—
Question 6.	760	767	736	278	641–42,
Interpreting the Map					
Question 1.	rear endpaper	767	rear endpaper	—	—
Question 2.	761, 764–65, 778	—	745, 746	277–282	—
Question 3.	769	775	740	280	644

Chapter 11: African-American Migration

	Martin, et. al.	Nash/Jeffrey	Divine, et. al.	Wilson, et. al.	Garraty
Mapping America					
Question 1.	—	—	—	—	—
Question 2.	—	—	—	—	481
Question 3.	front endpaper	—	rear endpaper	—	481
Reading the Map					
Question 1.	—	—	—	314	—
Question 2.	—	—	—	—	—
Question 3.	—	816	—	—	—
Question 4.	776	816	751	283	—
Interpreting the Map					
Question 1.	776, 794	816	751	283	649
Question 2.	776	816	751	314–18	649, 650

Chapter 12: Europe Between the Wars

	Martin, et. al.	Nash/Jeffrey	Divine, et. al.	Wilson, et. al.	Garraty
Mapping America					
Question 1.	760, 785	—	736, 754	284	656
Question 2.	760, 785	—	736, 754	284	656
Question 3.	785, 863	—	754	—	656
Question 4.	785	—	754	284	656
Reading the Map					
Question 1.	784, 785	792	754	284	655, 656
Question 2.	760, 785	792	736, 754	278, 284	655, 656
Question 3.	760, 785	792	736, 754	278, 284	655, 656
Question 4.	760, 785	792	736, 754	278, 284	655, 656
Question 5.	760, 785	—	736, 754	278, 284	—
Question 6.	760, 785	—	736, 754	278, 284	656
Question 7.	760, 785	792	736, 754	278, 284	655, 656
Question 8.	760, 785	—	736, 754	278, 284	656
Interpreting the Map					
Question 1.	784	792	754	284	656
Question 2.	784, 785	792	753–54	—	656
Question 3.	783–84	792	753–54	281	655

Chapter 13. New Consumerism and Gender Roles: A 1920s Home

No correlations.

Chapter 14. World War II in Europe and North Africa

	Martin, et. al.	Nash/Jeffrey	Divine, et. al.	Wilson, et. al.	Garraty
Mapping America					
Question 1.	882	900	832	404	753
Question 2.	882, 885	900	832	404	753
Question 3.	882, 885	900	832	404	753
Question 4.	880, 882	900	832	404	753
Reading the Map					
Question 1.	880, 882	900	832	392, 404	745, 753
Question 2.	880, 882	900	832	392, 401–3, 404	753
Question 3.	882	900	832	404	740, 753, 754
Question 4.	882, 884–85	900, 902	832, 841	403, 404	753, 754
Question 5.	882	900	831, 832	404	753
Question 6.	881, 883	904	831, 843	402, 404	761–62
Question 7.	881, 882	900,	831, 832	404	753
Interpreting the Map					
Question 1.	881	898–900	831	402–3, 404	753, 754
Question 2.	881	900,	831	403, 404	754
Question 3.	884–85	900	841–42	—	—

Chapter 15: World War II in the Pacific

	Martin	Nash	Divine	Wilson	Garraty	
Mapping America						
Question 1.	887	899	833		385, 407	7 5 8
Question 2.	887	899	833	407	758	
Question 3.	887	899	833	407	758	
Question 4.	887	899	833	407	758	
Question 5.	887	899	833	407	758	
Reading the Map						

	Martin, et. al.	Nash/Jeffrey	Divine, et. al.	Wilson, et. al.	Garraty
Question 1.	887	899	833	407	758
Question 2.	887	899	833	407	758
Question 3.	887	899	833	407	758
Question 4.	887	899	833	407	758
Question 5.	887	899	833	406	758
Question 6.	886, 887	899	833	407	757, 758
Question 7.	887	—	831–32	406, 407	757
Interpreting the Map					
Question 1.	886–88	899	831–32	406–7	757–58
Question 2.	887	899	831–32, 833	407	757–58
Question 3.	—	—	—	—	—
Question 4.	886–92	881, 902	827, 831–34	407	757–58

Chapter 16: The Cold War in Europe

	Martin, et. al.	Nash/Jeffrey	Divine, et. al.	Wilson, et. al.	Garraty
Mapping America					
Question 1.	905	957	852	411	772
Question 2.	—	957	852	411	772
Question 3.	905	957	852	411	772
Question 4.	905	—	852	—	772
Question 5.	905	957	852	411	772
Reading the Map					
Question 1.	904, 905	957	852	410–11	772
Question 2.	903–4	952	851	—	762–63
Question 3.	906–7	954	854–55	411–12	771
Question 4.	—	955	855	412	—
Question 5.	909–10	955–56	857, 860	412	773
Question 6.	941–42	958	916	—	784
Question 7.	904–5	955–56	851–52	411	772
Interpreting the Map					
Question 1.	903–6	905	843	—	762–63
Question 2.	903–6	900, 949	832, 851–52	404, 410	762–63
Question 3.	906	954, 957	854–55	411	771

Chapter 17: The Korean War and the Cold War in Asia

	Martin, et. al.	Nash/Jeffrey	Divine, et. al.	Wilson, et. al.	Garraty
Mapping America					
Question 1.	887	960	833	385, 415	758
Question 2.	913	960	864	385, 415	776
Question 3.	913	960	864	415	776
Question 4.	913	960	864	415	776
Reading the Map					
Question 1.	910	959	862–63	385, 412	774, 775
Question 2.	910	959	862	407	775
Question 3.	913, rear endpaper	960	864, rear endpaper	385	758, 776
Question 4.	913	960	863, 864	415	776
Question 5.	914	960	863	414, 415	776
Question 6.	914	960	863	413–14	776
Question 7.	913, 914	960	863	413–14, 415	776
Interpreting the Map					
Question 1.	910–14	959–60	863	412	776
Question 2.	908–9, 913	958	861–64	—	775
Question 3.	914	—	863–64	415	—

Chapter 18: Population Changes in the Twentieth Century

	Martin, et. al.	Nash/Jeffrey	Divine, et. al.	Wilson, et. al.	Garraty
Mapping America					
Question 1.	936	917	889	—	—
Question 2.	989 (1980s)	923, 1093	—	—	—
Reading the Map					
Question 1.	—	923, 1093	—	—	—
Question 2.	989	922, 923, 1092, 1093	—	—	823
Question 3.	—	924	—	—	—
Question 4.	—	923, 1093	—	—	—
Question 5.	—	923, 1093	—	—	—
Question 6.	989	1093	—	—	—
Question 7.	—	923, 1093	—	—	—
Interpreting the Map					
Question 1.	936–37, 971–72, 981–84	921–22, 924–28	878–80, 1011–13	446, 602	823–25

Question 2.	936–38	916–18, 922–23, 926–28	888, 889, 1011–12	446, 602	768, 769, 823
Question 3.	970–992	1092–93	972	446, 596	—

Chapter 19: The Vietnam War

	Martin, et. al.	Nash/Jeffrey	Divine, et. al.	Wilson, et. al.	Garraty
Mapping America					
Question 1.	1010, 1015	982	926	493	803
Question 2.	1015	982	926	493	803
Question 3.	1015	982	926	493	803
Question 4.	1015	982	926	493	803
Reading the Map					
Question 1.	1015	982	926	493	803
Question 2.	1015	982	926	493	803
Question 3.	1015	982	—	493	803
Question 4.	1010, 1015	978, 982	913, 926	493	803
Question 5.	1013	980	926	492–93	803
Question 6.	1015	982	926	493	803
Interpreting the Map					
Question 1.	1009, 1015	978–80	924–28	494–95	803–4
Question 2.	1010, 1015, 1016, rear endpaper	—	928–29	494–95	—
Question 3.	1010	978	913	493	783

Chapter 20: Immigration, 1950–90

	Martin, et. al.	Nash/Jeffrey	Divine, et. al.	Wilson, et. al.	Garraty
Mapping America					
Question 1.	rear endpaper	1097	rear endpaper	—	—
Question 2.	—	1097	—	—	802
Reading the Map					
Question 1.	—	1097	1013	—	802
Question 2.	—	1097	1013	—	802
Question 3.	—	1097	—	—	802
Question 4.	—	1097	—	—	802
Question 5.	—	1093, 1097	—	588	802, 870
Question 6.	—	1097	—	—	802
Interpreting the Map					
Question 1.	—	1009, 1093	1013	635–36	801, 874–75
Question 2.	1100	1009, 1094, 1106–7	964–5, 986, 1013	635–36	786, 801, 870
Question 3.	—	1009, 1093	963, 1013	635–36	801, 870

Chapter 21: The United States and the Middle East

	Martin, et. al.	Nash/Jeffrey	Divine, et. al.	Wilson, et. al.	Garraty
Mapping America					
Question 1.	1094	963	rear endpaper	—	863
Question 2.	1094	963	—	—	863
Question 3.	1094	963	—	—	—
Question 4.	1094	963	—	—	863
Reading the Map					
Question 1.	1094	963	—	—	753, 784
Question 2.	1094	963	rear endpaper	—	863
Question 3.	1094, rear endpaper	963	rear endpaper	—	863
Question 4.	1094, rear endpaper	963	rear endpaper	—	863
Question 5.	1094, rear endpaper	963	rear endpaper	—	863
Question 6.	1094, rear endpaper	963	rear endpaper	—	863
Question 7.	1094	963	—	—	—
Question 8.	1094, rear endpaper	963	—	—	863
Question 9.	1105, 1108–10	1105	987, 996	647–48	876–77
Interpreting the Map					
Question 1.	—	962	—	—	784
Question 2.	942, 1094, rear endpaper,	962–63, 1105–6	915–16, 955–57, rear endpaper	647	783–84, 876
Question 3.	1108–10	—	—	—	—

Chapter 22: The United States, Central America, and the Caribbean

Mapping America	Martin, et. al.	Nash/Jeffrey	Divine, et. al.	Wilson, et. al.	Garraty
Question 1.	1101	714	735,987, rear endpaper	275	619
Question 2.	1101	714	735, 987, rear endpaper	—	619
Question 3.	1101	714	987	—	619
Reading the Map					
Question 1.	944	963	916	451	786
Question 2.	945	964	916	461	786
Question 3.	945, 1007–8	973	922	461	793
Question 4.	1007	973	922–23	462	794
Question 5.	—	975	924	—	—
Question 6.	748, 1101	714	735, rear endpaper	—	—
Question 7.	1097, 1101	—	964	551	—
Question 8.	1100, 1101	1107	964, 986	607	872
Question 9.	1100, 1101	1107	986	606	866
Question 10.	1101	—	986	—	—
Question 11.	1101	—	—	—	—
Question 12.	1101	1107–8	995	646	875
Interpreting the Map					
Question 1.	744–48, 1100–101	708–11, 771–73, 963–64, 1106–8	732–33, 734, 916, 921–24, 962–63, 964–65, 986–88, 995	267–76, 460–61, 606, 607	607–616, 617–20, 621–23, 786, 866, 872–73, 875
Question 2.	1100–101	1106–8	986–88	606	866, 872–73, 875
Question 3.	1097, 1105, 1108	—	964–65	—	—

Chapter 23: The End of the Cold War in Europe

Mapping America	Martin, et. al.	Nash/Jeffrey	Divine, et. al.	Wilson, et. al.	Garraty
Question 1.	rear endpaper	—	995	—	—
Question 2.	—	—	—	—	—
Reading the Map					
Question 1.	1104	1104	994, 995	646	874
Question 2.	—	—	—	—	—
Question 3.	—	—	—	—	—
Question 4.	910	949	856–57	—	775
Interpreting the Map					
Question 1.	1107	1102–5	996, 998	649–55	875, 876, 878, 880